LEARN TO PAINT
WATERCOLOUR
WITH THE EXPERTS

Alwyn Crawshaw

David Bellamy

Ron Ranson

Hazel Soan

This edition published in 2003 by Collins, an imprint of
HarperCollins*Publishers*
77–85 Fulham Palace Road
Hammersmith, London W6 8JB

Compilation edition first published in 2002,
by Collins, exclusively for WH Smith

First published by Collins in paperback as:
Learn to Sketch 1998
Learn to Paint Watercolour Landscapes 1999
Learn to Paint Skies in Watercolour 2000
Learn to Paint Vibrant Watercolours 2000

04 06 08 09 07 05 03
2   4   6   7   5   3   1

New compilation edition edited by Heather Thomas
Production of this compilation edition by SP Creative Design Ltd

A catalogue record for this book is available
from the British Library

ISBN 0 00 715355 4

Colour origination by Colourscan, Singapore
Printed and bound in Hong Kong

Page 1: **Walking the Dog**, *Ron Ranson*, 31 x 41 cm (12 x 16 in)
Page 3: **Sarlat, Dordogne, France**, *Alwyn Crawshaw*, 17 x 15 cm (7 x 6 in)
This page: **This is My Town**, *Hazel Soan*, 43 x 56 cm (17 x 22 in)
Opposite: **Crab Boats, Sheringham**, *Alwyn Crawshaw*, 20 x 30 cm (8 x 12 in)

Contents

Alwyn Crawshaw

▲ Alwyn Crawshaw sketching outdoors.

Successful painter, author and teacher, Alwyn Crawshaw was born at Mirfield, Yorkshire and studied at Hastings School of Art. He now lives in Norfolk with his wife June, who is also an artist.

A Fellow of the Royal Society of Arts, a member of the British Watercolour Society and Society of Equestrian Artists, Alwyn is also President of the National Acrylic Painters Association. As well as painting in watercolour, he also works in oil and acrylic. He chooses to paint landscapes, seascapes, buildings and anything else that inspires him. Heavy working horses and winter trees are frequently featured in his landscape paintings and may be considered his trademark.

Alwyn has written eight titles for the *Collins Learn to Paint* series. His other books for Collins include: *The Artist At Work* , *Sketching with Alwyn Crawshaw*, *The Half-Hour Painter*, *Alwyn Crawshaw's Watercolour Painting Course*, *Alwyn Crawshaw's Oil Painting Course*, *Alwyn Crawshaw's Acrylic Painting Course* , *Alwyn & June Crawshaw's Outdoor Painting Course* and *Collins You can Paint Watercolour.*

Alwyn has made seven television series: *A Brush with Art*, *Crawshaw Paints on Holiday*, *Crawshaw Paints Oils*, *Crawshaw's Watercolour Studio*, *Crawshaw Paints Acrylics*, *Crawshaw's Sketching & Drawing Course* and *Crawshaw Paints Constable Country*, and he has written a book to accompany each series.

Alwyn has been a regular guest on local and national radio and has also appeared frequently on television. In addition, his own television programmes have been shown worldwide, including the United States and Japan. He has made many successful videos on painting and is also a regular contributor to the *Leisure Painter* magazine. Alwyn and June organize their own successful and extremely popular painting courses and holidays. They co-founded the Society of Amateur Artists, of which Alwyn was the President for several years.

Alwyn's paintings are sold in British and overseas galleries and can be found in private collections throughout the world. His work has been favourably reviewed by the critics. *The Telegraph Weekend Magazine* reported him to be 'a landscape painter of considerable expertise' and the *Artists and Illustrators* magazine described him as 'outspoken about the importance of maintaining traditional values in the teaching of art'.

David Bellamy

David Bellamy grew up in Pembrokeshire, Wales, where the natural environment had a profound effect on him. While he was working in the computer industry, he became drawn to climbing mountains. The sheer beauty of the wild environment enthralled him and he began taking a sketchbook and watercolour paints on his trips. Battling against rain, wind and snow, especially in winter, proved an interesting challenge – the watercolour sketches would often end up with the saturated pages stuck together, forming a damp mess in his rucksack! Now and then a real gem appeared, usually with a little help from nature, and this encouraged him to persevere.

These experiences proved invaluable in learning how to combine the elements, sky, atmosphere and the mountains themselves in a painting. A sense of atmosphere is often a dominant feature of his work.

After some successful exhibitions, he abandoned computing to concentrate on his painting. His first book, *Wild Places of Britain,* was followed by several art instruction books, including the bestselling *David Bellamy's Watercolour Landscape Course, Developing Your Watercolours, Learn to Paint Watercolour Landscapes* and many how-to-paint videos. He also writes about the country-side, contributes to *Leisure Painter* magazine and runs watercolour painting courses.

David has made several television series for HTV relating to art and the environment. His series, *Painting Wild Wales,* showed him painting and sketching climbing mountains, slithering down waterfalls and in caves and canyons. It is this first-hand involvement with the energy, vitality and beauty of his subject matter that inspires his best work.

▶ David Bellamy doing a rapid sketch in Mid Wales.

Ron Ranson

Born in Chesterfield, Ron Ranson's first career was in engineering. After an apprenticeship with Rolls Royce, he moved on to technical writing and illustration. Having always been interested in design, he entered the world of advertising, working as a visualizer. At the age of 38, he decided to change direction, became a publicity manager for an engineering firm and travelled the world, designing and erecting exhibition stands. After 12 years, he was back in the job market and this change marked the beginning of what became an incredible success story.

Ron decided to take a chance and break into the world of art. Specializing in watercolour, his paintings sold almost immediately. He soon discovered latent skills in teaching and writing and his career was established. He launched 'Wye Valley Watercolour Weekends', which attracted students from all over the world.

Having written for *Leisure Painter* magazine, Ron took the articles to a publisher who commissioned him to write *Watercolour Painting – The Ron Ranson Technique*. The book became a best seller world-wide, and so another aspect of his career was born. A prolific writer, he now has over 25 titles to his credit, including *Watercolour Landscapes from Photographs* and *Collins Learn to Paint Skies in Watercolour*. A pioneer of the teaching video, his videos sell worldwide.

All this activity brought requests from students as far afield as Australia, America and South Africa for Ron to teach in their own countries, and so began his foreign workshop tours. Much of his current work is done in European countries, including Norway, Holland, Italy, Greece and France.

America welcomed Ron with open arms; his workshops there are always filled to capacity. However, according to Ron, the best thing was that it produced his wife, Darlis, whom he met in Oregon on one of his painting workshops. In his usual dynamic way, he courted and married her, sweeping her off to England within two short months.

His *Australian Artist* magazine articles led to him being offered the prestigious position of European editor of the *International Artist Magazine* – a challenge he found impossible to refuse and which he held for several years.

▲ Ron Ranson at work on one of his dramatic skies.

Hazel Soan

▲ Hazel Soan painting in her London garden.

Hazel Soan was born in Surrey and began painting prolifically as a young teenager. At art college she realized that painting was her passion, and learning about living artists encouraged her to believe that she could earn a living from her art. The catalyst was a confidential report at college which read: 'Hazel has schoolgirl enthusiasm and romantic ideals about being an artist.' Rising to the challenge, she arranged her first exhibition soon after graduating. She sold nothing, but, undaunted, she rented a studio and continued to paint in between working behind the bar at a local pub. A patron suggested a London gallery she should approach and soon she had another exhibition. However, this time her watercolours sold out within the first hour. Her career was launched.

Since then Hazel has exhibited widely and has numerous one-woman shows to her credit. She has her own gallery in West London. Her paintings, both oils and watercolours, are collected by private and corporate buyers throughout the world. Several international hotels display her work, including the Ritz in London, and Sotheby's and Christie's have auctioned her paintings.

Hazel enjoys writing and she wants to encourage more people to experience the thrill of painting and shed their fears. She contributes regularly to art magazines and has published several art instruction books, including *Collins Watercolour Flower Painting Workshop*, *Learn to Paint Vibrant Watercolours* and *What Shall I Paint?*

She has made a number of instructional painting videos, several of which accompany her books, as well as filming two TV series for Anglia called *A Splash of Colour*. In recent years, she has become very well-known as one of the resident art experts on the very popular Channel 4 TV series *Watercolour Challenge*.

Hazel travels widely and divides her studio time between London and Cape Town.

Hazel lives through her eyes, seeing potential paintings everywhere. Despite her success and the thousands of pictures that she has produced, she still admits to feeling trepidation before a piece of white paper. It is this constant challenge and the desire to make images of what excites her visually that keeps her paintings vibrant.

Introduction

People often say, "I can't paint but I wish I could." But how many have ever tried or been taught to paint? Like any other art or trade, you have to learn in order to progress, and this book will introduce you to the wonderful world of watercolour painting.

Painting is one of man's earliest and most basic forms of expression – ever since Stone Age man drew on his cave walls. Since its primitive origins over 25,000 years ago, painting has become very sophisticated, and artists' materials have been transformed. Watercolour has become a popular medium which lends itself to painting a wide range of subjects. It requires no complicated equipment, making it ideal for a beginner. Even when painting outdoors, all you need are a pencil, paints, a brush, paper and water.

Start by sketching

The sketch is the beginning of almost any watercolour painting, and before you start to paint you need to make a preparatory sketch.

A sketch can be done for your own enjoyment or for collecting information, detail, mood or atmosphere to be used later as the basis for a finished studio painting. A sketch of a specific place will enable you to record what you see and feel. It is also an effective training exercise for drawing and painting which will make you more observant and open your eyes to new sights. You will 'see' things in a new light.

▲ **Sunny Morning, Winter 1998**
Ron Ranson
27 x 34 cm (10½ x 13 in)

▼ **Welly Weather**
Alwyn Crawshaw
38 x 50 cm (15 x 20 in)

You could even look at a telegraph pole and wonder at its beauty! So sketching is good preparation for planning your painting in watercolours, and it can help teach you the basics of design and composition and getting perspective into your painting.

Artists use the word 'sketch' in so many different ways, and a quick sketch can mean anything from an object that is carefully observed and portrayed with only a few pencil lines, to a watercolour painting that has not made the grade in the artist's eyes. They then say: "It's just a quick sketch!", using it as an excuse to cover up a poor painting!

Some artists take only a sketchbook and pencil with them when they go out sketching, while others take everything they can think of – easel, canvases, paints, seat, small table, umbrella, etc. Basically, what they really mean is that they are going out to draw or paint a picture and they might end up with a finished watercolour painting instead of a quick watercolour sketch.

There are four types of sketches. The first type is an *enjoyment sketch*, which is a drawing or a watercolour painting worked on location, done simply to enjoy the experience.

The second type is an *information sketch*. This is a drawing or painting done solely to collect information or detail, which can be used later at home or in the studio to create a more detailed and finished watercolour.

The third type is an *atmosphere sketch*. This is a drawing or painting worked specifically to get atmosphere and mood into the finished result. It can then be used later for creating atmosphere and mood information, or as the basis for an indoor painting.

▲ **Applecross Mountains**
David Bellamy
16 x 22 cm (6 x 9 in)

◀ **The Colour of Speed**
Hazel Soan
18 x 15 cm (7 x 6 in)

**▲ River Test,
Hampshire**
David Bellamy
13 x 28 cm (5 x 11 in)

The fourth type is a *specific sketch*, which is a drawing or painting of a certain subject to gather as much detailed information as possible but which also conveys the mood and atmosphere of the occasion. This sketch is used later as the basis for a finished painting.

All sketches, whether they are quick drawings or watercolour paintings, can be used as 'finished' works of art.

Watercolour landscapes

Having mastered the basic techniques of sketching in pencil and in watercolours, you will want to move on to watercolour painting and you can begin producing competent landscapes very quickly. It is best to start in a simple way and gradually build up to more complicated scenes, trying out techniques as

**▶ Low Clouds
Over the Estuary**
Ron Ranson
29 x 40 cm (11½ x 15½ in)

you progress. By practising each technique several times, you will become more adept at it and your confidence will grow.

Going out to work directly from nature is the best thing that a landscape artist can do. When you feel ready and in need of fresh material, just venture out in search of new subjects. The types of subject that you gravitate towards are important in your development as an artist. Finding what excites you most is vital as a source of inspiration.

Skies in watercolour

Skies are one of the most neglected areas of landscape painting, yet the sky is not only an integral part of the landscape but it also affects the whole scene below it. By creating authentic skies, you will learn new skills and add vitality, excitement and mood to your watercolour paintings, which will give endless satisfaction to you and your viewers.

Weather conditions can change a picture dramatically, even though the main subject and features remain the same. By learning about the basic cloud types, you can master the techniques that are needed to paint them and achieve atmospheric skies that will enhance the whole of your landscape painting.

The techniques for painting skies are easily learned, and watercolour is the ideal medium. The secret lies in the water content of your brush, and this practical exercise can be learned quickly and simply. There is nothing like the pleasure of watching an authentic watercolour sky materializing in front of your eyes. The other important thing to learn is when to stop. Overworking a painting can produce muddy, tired skies. With practice, you'll soon be painting successful skies.

Vibrant watercolours

These watercolours sing out from the page, making you feel good and seducing you with their bold impact and wonderful techniques. They are a delight to behold and a joy for you, the artist, to paint. To the novice, they look

▲ **Out of the Blue**
Hazel Soan
53 x 43 cm (21 x 17 in)

difficult but the secret is in knowing what watercolour can do, and then having the confidence to use that knowledge. When you are learning how to use watercolours you can sometimes try so hard that your frustration shows in your paintings and they become lacklustre, losing their spontaneity. However, you can learn how to make your paintings vibrant. By choosing a subject you really like and being relaxed, you can create a successful watercolour. The different techniques are discussed later in this book. By learning how to master the main watercolour techniques and giving special attention to brush strokes and laying paint as well as examining the thought behind the painting, you can produce colourful paintings of which you can feel justly proud. By using bold, lively colours with confidence, you can add an intensity and vibrancy to your work.

Materials and Equipment

Every professional artist has his or her favourite brushes, colours and so on. In the end, the choice must be left to you, to make from your personal experience. However, you actually need very few materials to make effective watercolour paintings. The less you have to carry and think about, the more likely you are to succeed in making your paintings work.

The only essential materials you require are some pencils or pens and ink for sketching, brushes, a paintbox or a few colours and a palette, paper, water and a rag. Depending on the size at which you choose to work, these items can fit into a small light bag or even a large pocket if you are working outside.

As you gain confidence you will inevitably want to try out more colours and different shaped or sized brushes. You may also want to work on larger paintings. However, most artists recommend that you use the minimum of equipment to start with and gradually build up, adding more as you find the need.

Paints

To get the best results, you should use the best materials you can afford. The two main distinctions between different watercolour paints are cost and quality. The best-quality watercolours are called 'artists' quality' paints whereas the lower grade ones are referred to as 'students' watercolours'. The artists' colours are made with ground pigments and will create the most vibrant colours and tonal variations. Students'

▲ Your basic painting equipment will most probably consist of a paint box filled with pans of colour, some tubes of paint, a few brushes, a porcelain palette with several compartments, water jars and some rag or tissue for blotting.

colours are made with cheaper pigments and are less intense, but they are also less expensive for you to buy.

Watercolours come in various forms, and both pans and tubes are available in the artists' and students' ranges. As a beginner, you may prefer to use the cheaper students' quality at first, later progressing to artists' quality as your confidence grows and your paintings improve. By this time, you will also have discovered the colours you prefer to use, and it will be worthwhile upgrading. Of course, both types are fully interchangeable and can be used together.

Watercolour paints can be bought in a watercolour box, filled with colours, or in separate pans which you can use as refills or to fill an empty box with your own choice of colours. In the pans, the watercolour is in solid form. Pans are compact and handy for sketching on location, especially when using small brushes. However, they can inhibit the use of large brushes and it is so tempting to dip into a whole variety of colours as they lay before you in their pans. This impulse dipping is not conducive to good watercolour practice.

If you prefer using tubes of paint, you have to squeeze the colour on to the palette (the open lid of the box). Colours in tubes are thick and fluid – ideal for quickly saturating a brush in strong colour, using less water, but they may not be best for all beginners because it is difficult to control the amount of paint that is picked up by the brush.

Perhaps the best solution is to have a basic palette of colours supplemented with tubes for the colours you use most often.

Choosing your colours

You do not need to buy a lot of colours. You only need about six or seven basic colours for each painting. Different artists have their own preferences, and as you experiment you will discover the colours that work best for you. One way to choose your selection is to find an artist's work you admire and copy their list of colours. If you buy a ready-made palette, the

French Ultramarine

Crimson Alizarin

Yellow Ochre

Hooker's Green No. 1

Cadmium Yellow Pale

Cadmium Red

Coeruleum

Burnt Umber

Payne's Grey

▲ The nine colours illustrated above are all suitable for beginners and can be used as the basis for almost any painting. However, you may wish to try other colours, too, especially for painting landscapes and skies, such as Raw Sienna, Burnt Sienna and Cobalt Blue. Please note that this colour chart is produced within the limitations of printing and it is intended as a guide only.

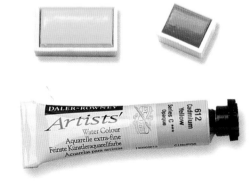

◄ You can buy watercolour paints in half pans, whole pans and tubes. Each has its own advantages.

choice of colours is usually made for you, but you can fill empty palettes with pans or select your own tubes. It is best to limit yourself to a few well-chosen pigments.

▲ A basic watercolour painting kit. The paper is stretched on a drawing board ready for painting. Note the tray-type palette (bottom left), which is ideal for mixing colours from tubes, and the small china mixing well (bottom). Many artists prefer to use half pans.

Brushes

The most important piece of equipment is the brush. It is the extension of your hand and eye when painting, and therefore it must be as sensitive and versatile as you. Brushes are the one item on which you should not economize, and you will need a range of sizes: large ones for washes of colour, smaller ones for more detailed areas, and a rigger for fine detail.

The best brushes are made of pure sable because they point well, have a spring to them and give you perfect control over your brush strokes. If they are properly cared for, they will last a long time and are worth the initial investment. Before buying, however, check that they come to a fine point by dipping them in water (which any good art shop should supply). Sables, being hand-made, are the most expensive type of brush, but there are now also many excellent synthetic ranges

on the market, including some sable/synthetic mixtures. Alternatively, there are less expensive fine-quality ranges of watercolour brushes which are made with squirrel hair, ox-ear hair and ringcat hair.

A good brush holds ample paint between the hairs in the body of the brush, yet even in the largest sizes has a tip that is capable of painting fine detail. Buy a size 7 round brush made of Kolinsky sable and see how broad a wash you can achieve and how fine a line you can draw with the same brush. If you plan to work small a size 5 will do, but if you work larger choose a size 10 or 12. Remember to check the quality of the tip when you buy a brush.

You can add to your brush collection flat brushes for creating broad washes and different brush marks, and some big cheap mops for distributing paint on a large scale. Squirrel hair mop brushes hold a lot of water, and they come in a variety of sizes. Buy the largest you feel happy with because the fewer strokes you use, the better and fresher your work will appear. Round brushes – Nos. 4, 8 and 12 in particular – are good to start with, plus a No. 1 rigger. This slender brush has long hairs and holds a lot of paint for its size. It is called a rigger as it was originally used for painting the rigging on ships.

Brush types

Because brushes are the tools with which you express yourself on paper and reveal your skills to the onlooker, it is important that you get to know your brushes and what to expect from them.

There are two basic types of brush:
• Round brushes
• Flat brushes.

The round brush is a general-purpose one: both a wash and a thin line can be obtained with this shape. Usually, round brushes are graded from size No. 00 to size No. 12, and some manufacturers make a No. 14 size. This scale can be seen in the picture (right).

The flat brush is used mainly for putting washes over large areas or where a broad brush stroke is called for. Naturally, the width of these strokes is determined by the size of the flat brush. Flat brushes and very large brushes, such as the squirrel-hair wash brush, have a name or size of their own.

Looking after brushes

It is very important that you look after your brushes. Always remember to rinse them out thoroughly after use with clean water and leave them to dry upright in a well-ventilated area out of direct sunlight. Never stand them resting on the brush hairs in your water pot.

▶ A selection of brushes for watercolours. All the brushes are shown actual size, and some brush series have additional sizes to those shown, i.e. Nos. 9, 11 and 14. However, you don't have to spend a fortune on pure sable brushes; the synthetic ranges, such as Dalon, are perfectly satisfactory, especially for beginners.

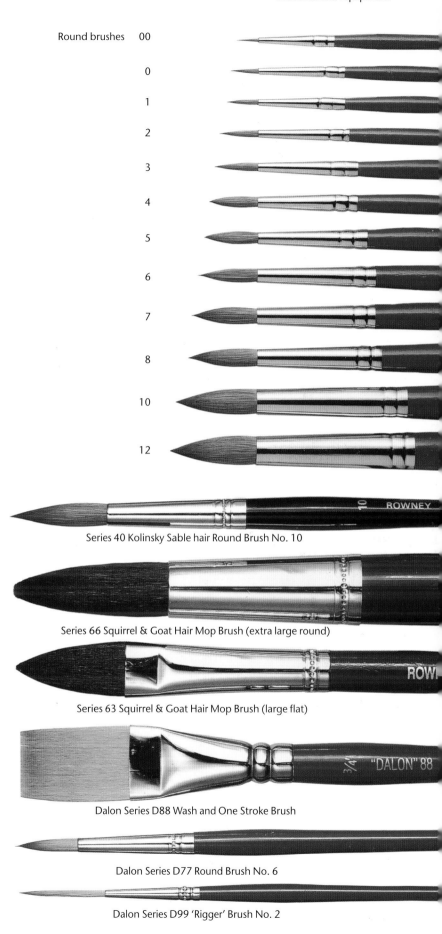

Round brushes 00

0

1

2

3

4

5

6

7

8

10

12

Series 40 Kolinsky Sable hair Round Brush No. 10

Series 66 Squirrel & Goat Hair Mop Brush (extra large round)

Series 63 Squirrel & Goat Hair Mop Brush (large flat)

Dalon Series D88 Wash and One Stroke Brush

Dalon Series D77 Round Brush No. 6

Dalon Series D99 'Rigger' Brush No. 2

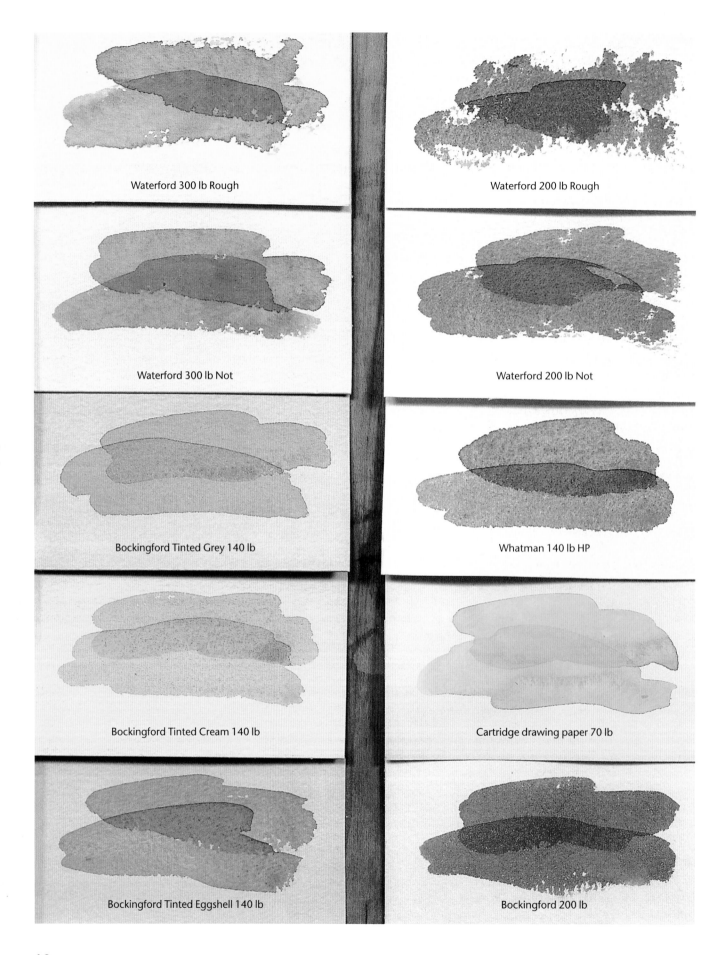

Waterford 300 lb Rough

Waterford 200 lb Rough

Waterford 300 lb Not

Waterford 200 lb Not

Bockingford Tinted Grey 140 lb

Whatman 140 lb HP

Bockingford Tinted Cream 140 lb

Cartridge drawing paper 70 lb

Bockingford Tinted Eggshell 140 lb

Bockingford 200 lb

Paper

Although you can use virtually any paper for painting with watercolours, the specially made watercolour papers are best. Their unique surface texture is sympathetic to the brush and this helps to create the unique watercolour effect. The paper also has just the right amount of absorbency to hold the liquid colour under manageable control. The finest-quality papers are still made by hand, by expert craftsmen whose skills have been handed down over centuries.

Watercolour papers are available in a wide range of different textures and weights, but they all have two things in common: they are all finished with one of three kinds of surface texture; and they are all graded by their weight. The surfaces are: Rough, Not and Hot Pressed.

Paper with a Rough surface has a very pronounced texture and is usually used for large paintings where bold, vigorous brush work is required. The Not surface has less texture, and this is the one most commonly used by artists. It is also ideal for beginners. The Hot Pressed surface is extremely smooth with very little texture. Before you try this paper, you will need to know how to handle your watercolour. If you use the paint very wet, it can easily run.

There are two other papers on which you can work: Bockingford watercolour paper, which has only one surface (similar to the Not surface), and cartridge drawing paper, which has only a smooth surface.

Usually you buy watercolour paper in sheets but you can also purchase it in pads or special watercolour blocks which are excellent for using when working out-of-doors.

Paper weights vary, the most common ones being 180 gsm (90 lb), 300 gsm (140 lb), 410 gsm (200 lb) and 640 gsm (300 lb). The most popular weight is 300 gsm (140 lb) but, unless you work on a very small scale, it needs stretching (see right), otherwise it may cockle badly when you put thin, wet paint on it.

To start with, get used to two or three types of paper. You will learn how the paper reacts to the paint and what you can and can't do. This is as important as getting used to your brushes and colours.

Other materials

As well as paints, brushes and paper, you will need at least one drawing board, a large palette or white saucer, a selection of pencils or sticks of charcoal to make preliminary sketches, some pens and coloured inks, a putty eraser, a water container, masking fluid, paper tissues and a rag or natural, soft sponge. A few Stanley-knife blades may also be useful for scratching away paint and for creating special effects in your paintings.

An easel is not essential – you can work very comfortably at a table, supporting the top edge of your drawing board with a book or piece of wood about 8–10 cm (3–4 in) high so the washes can run down correctly.

For sketching outdoors, remember to keep your equipment simple and start with just some pencils and a pad. However, you can buy folding easels and even collapsible water containers if you are really committed. The best advice is to travel light and only take a few paints and brushes you really need.

▶ To stretch paper and prevent it cockling, cut a sheet of paper which is slightly smaller than your drawing board. Either submerge it in water or hold it under a running cold tap and completely soak both sides. Hold the sheet of paper up by one end, let the surface water drain off and then lay it on the drawing board. Use a roll of brown gummed paper to stick the four sides down, allowing the gummed paper to fall half over the paper and half over the board. Leave it to dry naturally overnight and by morning it will be as tight as a drum and as flat as a pancake, and will stay perfectly flat while you work. The finished result is shown here.

Sketching for Watercolour
By Alwyn Crawshaw

The sketch is the beginning. Almost all work that has been created on paper, canvas, clay, stone, metal, or indeed any artist's medium, started as a sketch. To paint effective watercolours, you need to plan your painting and sketch it out in advance. An idea can be stimulated by a thousand things, but a sketch can hold it for all time and be used as a foundation for other work, even though the idea may represent only a fleeting moment of inspiration. You should never throw a sketch away, no matter how small or insignificant you think it is. You have created something unique and original from which you can always learn or work from, even years later.

Seeing things differently

In this book, I want to teach you how to sketch out of doors and how to use your sketches either as works in their own right or as training exercises for watercolour painting. This will enable you to build on the knowledge you already have or, if you are a beginner, will open your eyes to new sights that can be experienced only when you look around you with sympathetic and observant eyes. You will 'see' things in a new light.

I want you to be able to go out with confidence and enjoy your sketching. I enjoy sketching just as much, or even more

▲ Spring Sunlight, Saltham, Norfolk
2B pencil and watercolour on cartridge paper
28 x 40 cm (11 x 16 in)

sometimes, than sitting in my studio painting a 'masterpiece' (my interpretation!). One of the greatest advantages is that sketching provides a reason to go outdoors and enjoy your surroundings.

What is a sketch?

Let's get back to the drawing board. We know that a sketch is the beginning, but what exactly is meant by the word 'sketch'? It can be used in so many different ways. I have defined the word from the artist's point of view and, after a lot of careful thought, I have broken down the sketch into four distinct and practical types.

1 Enjoyment sketch. This is a drawing or painting worked on location, done simply to enjoy the experience.

2 Information sketch. This is a drawing or painting which is done solely to collect information or detail. It can be used later at home or in the studio.

3 Atmosphere sketch. This is a drawing or painting done specifically to introduce mood into the finished result. It can be used later for evoking atmosphere or as the inspiration for an indoor painting.

4 Specific sketch. This is a drawing or a painting done of a specific subject to gather as much detailed information as possible, but which also conveys the mood and atmosphere of the occasion. The sketch is used as the basis for a finished painting.

You may have a preconceived idea of what type of sketch you are going to do. However, if you don't know what to draw, then empty your mind completely of what you thought you might do and start looking around at what is available. Usually you will then see your surroundings totally differently and can find an inspiring subject.

Points to remember

Important information to note down on your sketch are things such as the position of the sun and shadows, the sizes and positions of important areas, such as a boat, a building or a tree, and their position in relation to each other. Also, make sure you put something in your sketch to give an idea of the scale. If you are working in black and white, then you will need to make colour notes for when you do a watercolour painting later.

However, when you make a watercolour sketch, don't put any comments or coding on it. Because of the relaxed manner in which it is approached, this type of sketch can often turn out to be a perfect watercolour painting. If you need to record some information, write your notes lightly on the back in pencil, or on another piece of paper.

◀ **Exmouth Harbour**
2B pencil on cartridge paper
17 x 28 cm (7 x 11 in)

Simple Perspective

You don't need to know everything about perspective to be able to paint or sketch a picture. But I believe, your sketching will become easier and the result more convincing if you know the basics of perspective.

When you look out to sea the horizon will always be at your eye level, whether you are on a clifftop or lying flat on the sand. So the horizon is the eye level (EL). Of course, if you are in a room there is no horizon, but you still have an eye level. To find it, hold a pencil horizontally in front of your eyes at arm's length. Your eye level is where the pencil hits the opposite wall. If two parallel lines were marked out on the ground and extended to the horizon, they would come together at what is called the vanishing point (VP). This is why railway lines appear to get closer together and finally meet in the distance – they have met at the vanishing point.

The basic rules

The page opposite really isn't as complicated as it looks. Let's go through it in stages. I started by drawing a straight line across to represent the eye level (EL). You should do the same. Next draw the red square shown in fig. **1**. Put a mark to the left at eye level, and use it as your vanishing point (VP). Then start to turn the square into a cube by drawing lines from the VP to both its left-hand corners. You can see that, having reached the same stage in fig. **2**, I've then joined up the right-hand corners to the VP to form two sides.

Copying my fig. **3**, draw a line between the top and bottom guidelines parallel to the left side of the square (see points **a** and **b**). This gives one side of a box . Then draw a horizontal line from point **a** to link with the guideline on the other side of the box at point **c**, and the same again, starting at **b** and drawing a horizontal line to the lower guideline at point **d**. Finally, join up points **c** and **d** with a perpendicular line. You will now have a cube and have succeeded in representing a three-dimensional object on a two-dimensional surface (your paper) with basic perspective theory using eye level and vanishing point.

In fig **4**, I have turned the cube into a house, by adding a roof. To find the centre of a square or cube, whatever its proportions, draw two diagonal lines from corner to corner. Where they converge is the centre. From this point I drew a guideline up to meet another line drawn from the VP to the point of the roof. Where these two lines cross is the apex of the roof. The house has two vanishing points, one on the left and one on the right. The principle is the same as for the first cube you drew, except the lines on both sides of the cube meet at a vanishing point.

I have drawn a 'bird's eye view' in fig **5**, by putting the eye level higher. Fig. **6** is just the opposite – a 'worm's eye view'. The eye level is very low, in fact, at ground level. Parallel lines meet at the VP and this includes windows, windowsills, doors, gutters, pavements, the line of lampposts – everything!

Please read this page very carefully and practise. It will help you to 'see' perspective when you are sketching.

When out sketching, find your eye level by holding your pencil horizontally at arm's length in front of your eyes. Then draw it in on your sketchpad, position your centre of interest and work from there.

▶ Practise the work opposite. Try drawing houses with your eye level at different heights and the vanishing points in different positions. This will quickly help you to understand this basic rule of perspective.

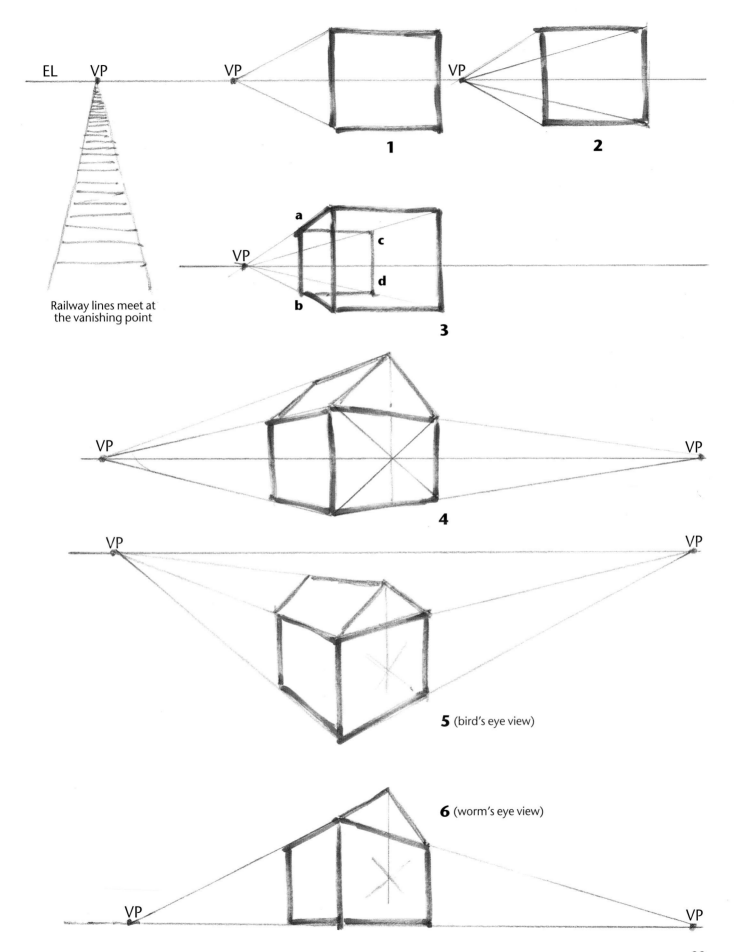

EL   VP

VP

VP

1

2

Railway lines meet at
the vanishing point

VP

a

c

b

d

3

VP

VP

4

VP

VP

5 (bird's eye view)

6 (worm's eye view)

VP

VP

Design and Composition

Design is so much a matter of personal observation, that it is difficult to say what is good or bad. We don't always know, when we like a picture, how much the design and composition influence us. It may be the subject or the colours that attract us but, as far as sketching is concerned, take it from simple beginnings and let your instinct guide you with the help of some basic rules.

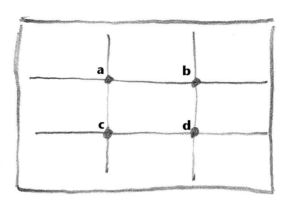

◀ Divide your picture into thirds, **a**, **b**, **c**, and **d** are the focal points.

Basic rules

I have called this section Design and Composition because to me, in painting, they mean the same thing, namely: the positioning of objects on paper in a 'happy' way that enables you to tell a story visually to the onlooker. Let us start with a very old system that I was taught at art school, which is now second nature to me. Although it is a good rule of thumb to work to, do not be stereotyped into sticking rigidly to rules. We are all individuals and a deviation from the expected to a more personal choice can make an original and sometimes unusual picture.

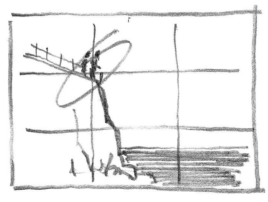

◀ In this sketch the centre of interest is positioned at focal point **d**. This is good.

Focal points

In each of the illustrations *(right)*, I have divided the paper into thirds, vertically and horizontally. Where they cross at points **a**, **b**, **c** and **d**, I have called the focal points.

If your centre of interest is positioned on or around a focal point as in the second sketch, then you should have a good design.

Look at the two people standing on the cliff in the third sketch and you will see that the composition looks 'happy'. (By that I mean it works well.)

Now look at the fourth sketch, where the two figures are still on the cliff, but now in the centre of the picture. It looks uninteresting and characterless.

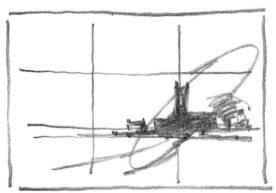

◀ The two people are positioned at focal point **a**. This is good too.

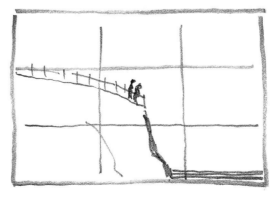

◀ These two people are in the centre of the picture. This is not good composition.

Starting at the centre of interest

When you are composing a landscape or seascape, always have the horizon above or below the centre of the paper, never in the middle. Start by putting in your centre of interest at your chosen focal point, then work away from it. You will find that nature's lines, if observed carefully – hedgerows, rivers, roads and so on – will help to bring the picture together and form a natural design.

Making a picture finder

If your subject is large, such as a landscape or a village square and you can't decide which part to sketch, cut a mask out of thin card with an opening of about 10 x 8 cm (4 x 3 in). Hold up your masking card (picture finder) at arm's length and look, with one eye closed, through the mask 'window', see the illustration *(right)*. Move it around slowly up and down and backwards and forwards until you see a 'picture' that fires your imagination. Make mental notes of where your arm is and where the key points of the scene hit the edge of the mask. Mark these on your sketchpad and away you go!

Eventually design will come naturally as you progress and develop your own style, and the more you sketch the sooner your design will become second nature.

Collecting information

My little sketch of Val André *(below right)* shows the advantage of drawing plenty of information onto your sketch. Although the sketch is very simple, it gives me enough information to be able to work from at home – enough for two different pictures, in fact, with different centres of interest!

▶ This illustration shows two interesting ways of using one sketch. The blue outline shows the island as the centre of interest. The red outline gives a different view, with the two main foreground figures as the centre of interest. If I painted using the second outline, I would use strong local colour to emphasise the figures as the island could be overpowering.

▶ These little sketches show simple designs using different focal points. The centre of interest can always be made to stand out from its immediate surroundings – for example, you can use contrast when working in black and white, or vivid or different colours when you are working in colour. This is good.

▼ A picture finder will help you to decide which part of a landscape to paint. This is good, too.

Working in Pencil

The most important piece of sketching equipment is the pencil. We tend to take the pencil for granted and it is not surprising. We all have one, somewhere. A good artist's drawing pencil has 13 different degrees of lead. The middle one, and the most common for everyday use, is HB. For general sketching purposes I use a 2B, which is a softer pencil, and sometimes a 3B, which is softer still.

Your basic sketching kit

All you need to get started are a 2B pencil, a putty eraser and a sketchpad. For me, this is the most versatile and pleasant way to sketch. It is also the least expensive. At least 60 per cent of my outdoor sketching is done with a pencil on an A4 or A3 cartridge paper sketchpad. You can also use a pad of layout paper. This is a strong, thin paper which has a good surface for pencil work. It is also less expensive than cartridge paper and is therefore excellent for practising.

Staying sharp

It is important to get the most out of your pencil and the first thing to learn is how to sharpen it to get the best results. Use a sharp knife and cut off controlled positive slices, making a long, gradual taper to the lead.

A putty eraser is a very important part of an artist's sketching kit. Always keep one handy and never be afraid to use it for rubbing out!

▲ Basic pencil sketching set.

◄ Use a sharp knife to sharpen your pencil to give a long point.

◄ The first pencil is sharpened to a point. The second one is sharpened to a flat chisel-shaped end which is good for shading. The third pencil is sharpened badly and would be difficult to draw with. I borrowed it from one of my new students!

◄ To protect pencil points, secure them to a piece of thick card with rubber bands, or make a cover for the lead by rolling some cartridge paper around the pencil and winding masking tape around it.

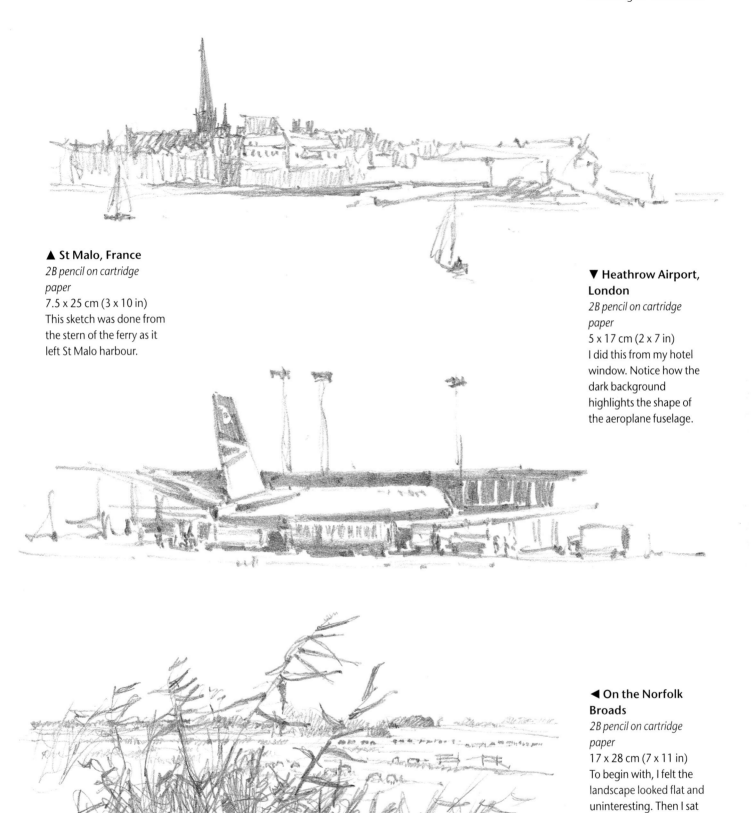

▲ St Malo, France
2B pencil on cartridge paper
7.5 x 25 cm (3 x 10 in)
This sketch was done from the stern of the ferry as it left St Malo harbour.

▼ Heathrow Airport, London
2B pencil on cartridge paper
5 x 17 cm (2 x 7 in)
I did this from my hotel window. Notice how the dark background highlights the shape of the aeroplane fuselage.

◄ On the Norfolk Broads
2B pencil on cartridge paper
17 x 28 cm (7 x 11 in)
To begin with, I felt the landscape looked flat and uninteresting. Then I sat down and saw these long grasses and reeds blocking my view and was inspired so I sketched it. I know one day I will use this sketch to do a painting in my studio.

▲ 'Short' drawing position

▲ 'Long' drawing position

▲ 'Flat' drawing position

Holding your pencil

Most of us have used pencil or pens for writing since childhood and unfortunately, old habits die hard. To sketch successfully, you must learn to hold your tools for sketching in several different ways. In the photographs showing pencil holds you will see two types of arrow. The red arrow shows the direction of the pencil strokes, and the blue arrow shows the direction in which the pencil is travelling over the paper. I use these arrows throughout the book.

The 'short' drawing position
The way one holds a pencil for writing is fine for controlled drawing and careful line work.

The 'long' drawing position
However, for a more free and flowing movement, especially needed in working the sketch over a large area, you must hold your pencil at least 7.5 cm (3 in) from the point and have the pencil at a flatter angle to the paper. This 'long' drawing position (see the second example) will give more versatility to the pencil strokes.

The 'flat' drawing position
This is a totally different way of holding your pencil. The pencil is almost flat on the paper, held off by your thumb and first finger, which allows you to touch and move over the surface. This way of working your pencil allows you to work in fast broad strokes, using the long edge of the lead to give large shaded areas.

Doodle to practise!
With these three positions there are infinite variations. Using these as a base, learn to work with a pencil, all over again. Practise whenever you can – doodle, do anything. Don't worry about drawing, just get used to the pencil and what you can make it create on paper. Don't worry about rubbing anything out, either. Taking away what you don't want is as important as putting your drawing in.

These sketches were drawn on cartridge paper twice the size they are reproduced here. I did the one above at a local point-to-point meeting. The one on the left was done at the Blackpool Tower Ballroom and the sketch below became a demonstration for students during a coffee break on a painting holiday in France.

▲ Here I have shown the tonal ranges of a 2B pencil (on the left) and a 3B pencil (on the right).

Working in Pen and Ink

For basic ink sketching, you need a sketching pad and a pen. But which pen should you choose? The thickness of the nib, and the line it creates, is very much a matter of personal preference, as is the general design of the pen. Look for one that feels well-balanced and is comfortable to draw with. Also make sure that it is waterproof so that, should you decide to turn your drawing into a pen and wash painting, you will be able to paint over your pen marks without any fear of them running. Pen and wash is a versatile medium which can be adapted to any style and can create diverse effects in your watercolour paintings. The wide range of coloured inks can add tone, texture and contrast to your watercolour paintings.

Dip-in pens!

A mapping pen has a nib with a very fine point and is used universally for fine pen drawings. You can buy various types of drawing nibs – all 'dip-in-ink' pens – so you must take a bottle of waterproof drawing ink with you when sketching. Experiment with different nibs and get the feel of working with them. Don't be afraid of them: they are more flexible and stronger than you imagine, but if you press hard on an upstroke you could damage the nib. You need a hard surface paper or board for fine nib work.

> A pen is a good medium to teach you to sketch decisively – the more you practise, the more positive your drawings will become.

▲ My basic ink sketching kit contains a sketchpad, some waterproof ink, a mapping pen, ballpoint pen and a Uni-Ball Signo marker pen.

Easier options

Nowadays, drawing marker pens, with varying nib sizes, are used by many artists. They are more convenient because you do not have to dip them in ink. For all my outdoor pen sketching, I use this type of marker pen – normally either a Uni-Ball Signo or Uni Pin Fine Line Marker.

Try using a ballpoint pen as well. The results can look a little mechanical, but there are quite a few advantages. It is inexpensive, you don't have to dip it in ink or fill it, and you usually have one in your pocket. It definitely makes a very good standby sketching tool in an emergency.

▲ I did all these sketches from the same sitting position, in my A4 cartridge sketchpad. I don't think that dog at the top liked me!

◄ This sketch was drawn on Ivorex board 12 x 20 cm (4¾ x 8 in). I feel the fence stabilises the sketch – the lines for it were drawn freely but carefully.

Exercises in Black and White

Now that you have experimented with black and white sketching materials, we can try some very simple exercises. I have done these in stages to show you how I work.

The first two exercises will help you develop a broad pencil treatment. Use your 3B pencil and hold it in the 'flat' drawing position (see page 28) to give you broad shading for the tonal work.

Start the exercise below by drawing in the line of the field, then put in the buildings (the centre of interest), and follow my stages. Then try the next exercise. Don't labour your pencil work – make your pencil work freely, trying for light against dark (strong contrast)

with shading. Then try the last sketch.

You can try any of these exercises using other black and white mediums and this will help you to see which subject suits which medium. For instance, it would be difficult to get the atmosphere in the second exercise (right) if you used a fine nib pen. The sky would be scratchy and difficult to make very black, but it would work well with charcoal.

These exercises should be useful. They will have made you copy something, which will help you to observe nature when you are out sketching. The more you sketch, the more confidence you will have so, whenever you have ten minutes to spare – *sketch*!

▼ I did this exercise on layout paper 15 x 15 cm (6 x 6 in) with a 3B pencil. Use your pencil in a 'flat' drawing position for the shaded areas. Although this is a very simple sketch, and worked without detail, the strong contrast between dark and light areas makes it work.

◄ This is another simple sketch to help you with shading. I did it on layout paper, 15 x 15 cm (6 x 6 in) using a 3B pencil. The shading of the dark sky is important. Again, hold your pencil in the 'flat' drawing position to do this. Notice how the angle of the shading changes as it nears the horizon and the shading becomes darker. I did this to add drama to the scene.

► This small sketch was done on layout paper, 9 x 12.5 cm (3½ x 5 in) with a 2B pencil. Follow the stages carefully. Of course, if I were to do a similar sketch of this house again from the same spot, on a different day, I might not start it in exactly the same way! That is the nature of sketching – as you gain experience, you will find that your feeling for each subject will dictate how you tackle it on the day.

33

Working in Watercolour

Over the next few pages, I hope to take some of the mystery out of using watercolour. This theme will be developed in more detail throughout this book by myself and the other contributors.

But first let us take a look at colour. It can make us happy, it can give the effect of cold, warmth, dark or light, and yet all the colours that we paint with are made up from only three basic colours: red, yellow and blue. These are called the 'primary' colours. I have listed the colours that I use below, in order of their importance to me.

Mixing colours

The next stage is to learn how to mix colours. On the next page you will see that I have mixed primary colours to make other colours. In watercolour painting you use more water and less paint to make your colours lighter. To make them darker, you need to use more paint and less water. I don't use black, only because I was taught not to, because it is a 'dead' colour. If you *mix* a black (as shown opposite) it is much more alive than any ready-made black.

Watercolour is a good medium to learn to paint with. Firstly, whether we were artistic or

Always carry your sketchbook in a plastic bag when you are working outside. I once ruined all my watercolour sketches by dropping my unprotected sketchbook in a puddle!

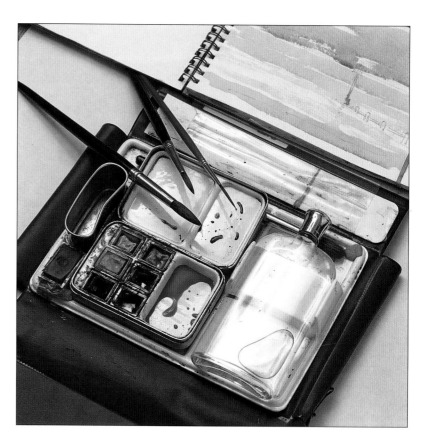

▲ My basic watercolour sketching kit is my Watercolour Travelling Studio, which I designed many years ago for easy working outdoors *(see left)*. This contains a paintbox with six colours, a water bottle, water container, brush, pencil and a 13 x 28 cm (5 x 7 in) sketchpad. Lightweight and waterproof, it has a carrying strap which also supports it around your neck when you are standing to work. I rest my A4 or A3 sketchpad on it when working larger. My brushes are Nos. 10 and 6 round sable and a Dalon Series D99 'Rigger' No. 2.

My colours

French Ultramarine, Crimson Alizarin, Yellow Ochre, Hooker's Green No. 1, Cadmium Yellow Pale, Cadmium Red and Coeruleum. I use the first four colours in about 80 per cent of my painting. I also, occasionally, use Burnt Umber and Payne's Grey.

not, most of us were taught to paint with water-based paints at school or even before, usually with poster paint (in jars) or powder paint (in tins, which had to be mixed with water). So a beginner to painting, at whatever his or her age, will not feel totally alien to watercolour paints, because at some time he or she will have come in contact with them.

Secondly, watercolour is a very convenient medium to use indoors to practise with. Getting out a box of watercolour paints and working in a corner of a room is relatively easy, and there is no smell.

Mixing colours is fun, so have a go and see what you get. The more difficult colours to mix are the subtler ones, and these will come with practice and observation.

Use the predominant colour first

Always start your mix with the predominant colour. If you are mixing a 'yellowy' orange, begin with yellow and add a little red. To mix a 'reddy' brown, you should start with red, then add a little yellow, and then a little blue. I have listed my colours for mixing in this way throughout the following pages.

Keep things simple

When you first go outside sketching with watercolour, go for broad areas, using colours that are simple to mix. Time and experience will extend your colour range.

When you are out in the country, look at the distant hills, covering up the foreground fields with your hands. Then look at the foreground fields. The colour in the distance is blue compared to the green of the foreground field. In general, the distance is bluish (cooler), and the foreground is warmer and has more real colour.

Look for these colour changes and observe them in your sketches and you will find that the background stays in the distance, and the foreground in front. Your sketches will then have meaning and come to life.

In general, to make your colours cooler (for distance), add blue, and to make them warmer (for foreground), add red.

Primary colours

Crimson Alizarin + Cadmium Yellow Pale = French Ultramarine

Mixing colours

Cadmium Yellow Pale + French Ultramarine = Green

Cadmium Yellow Pale + Crimson Alizarin = Orange

Crimson Alizarin + Cadmium Yellow Pale + French Ultramarine = Brown

French Ultramarine + Crimson Alizarin + Cadmium Yellow Pale = Black

Hooker's Green No. 1 — French Ultramarine

add Crimson Alizarin — add Crimson Alizarin

add more Crimson Alizarin — add more Crimson Alizarin

add water — add water

add French Ultramarine — add more water

add water — add French Ultramarine

In the colour mixing examples *(above)*, you will see that I have worked across, mixing primary colours to produce green, orange, brown and black. In the colour mixing examples *(left)*, I worked downwards, mixing colours together and also adding water to make the colours paler. Experiment and practise mixing colour on any paper that is available to you. Try printer paper, which is inexpensive – then you won't be worried about starting over and over again. Begin by mixing your colours just from the three primaries, because this will help you to understand colour mixing more easily. Good luck and have fun!

35

Exercises in Colour

Now that you have practised colour mixing, you will be ready to try some simple exercises. Don't let the exercises on these two pages worry you because they have shape and form, while you may only have experimented with coloured 'doodles' so far.

Simplifying objects

If you look at the small rowing boat on the opposite page, the first stage is really just a shapeless doodle of two colours and the second stage only gets its boat shape by adding one darker tone in the correct places. This comes from observation of your subject, but you can see how to simplify objects and still make them appear three-dimensional.

Take this a little further and look at the wheelbarrow below the rowing boat. As you gain confidence you will find that you can put the second tone in (the shadow side of the wheelbarrow) as you paint in the first stage. In other words, you would paint in the light area on two sides and then paint in the other two sides with a darker tone. In this way, you miss out a stage. When you are painting complicated subjects you will find that this happens throughout the picture.

Discovering short cuts

Concentrate on working simply at first. This is especially important when you are out sketching. If you find short cuts that enable you to work better, by all means use them. Painting is a very personal thing and, with experience, all artists develop their own special methods and techniques.

I did the sketches on the opposite page for you to copy on cartridge paper. I hope you enjoy doing them, as well as the step-by-step exercise on this page.

◄ I started by drawing this sketch with a 2B pencil on Bockingford paper, 15 x 15 cm (6 x 6 in). I used my No. 6 brush for the whole sketch, first painting in the sky using French Ultramarine and Crimson Alizarin. When this was dry, I used the same colours, but stronger, to paint in the distant hills. Notice how blue they are.

◄ When this was dry, I painted the distant trees with a mix of French Ultramarine, Crimson Alizarin and a little Yellow Ochre. I used a mix of Crimson Alizarin and Yellow Ochre for the autumnal foliage behind the large trees, then a varying mix of Cadmium Yellow Pale, Crimson Alizarin and a touch of Hooker's Green No. 1 for the fields.

◄ In the final stage, I painted in the large tree and the hedgerow and, when this was dry, painted autumn leaves over the branches. The same colour was used for the shadows on the river bank. Then, with the sky colour, I painted horizontal brush strokes to represent water. Finally, when the water was dry, I put in the reflections of the trees.

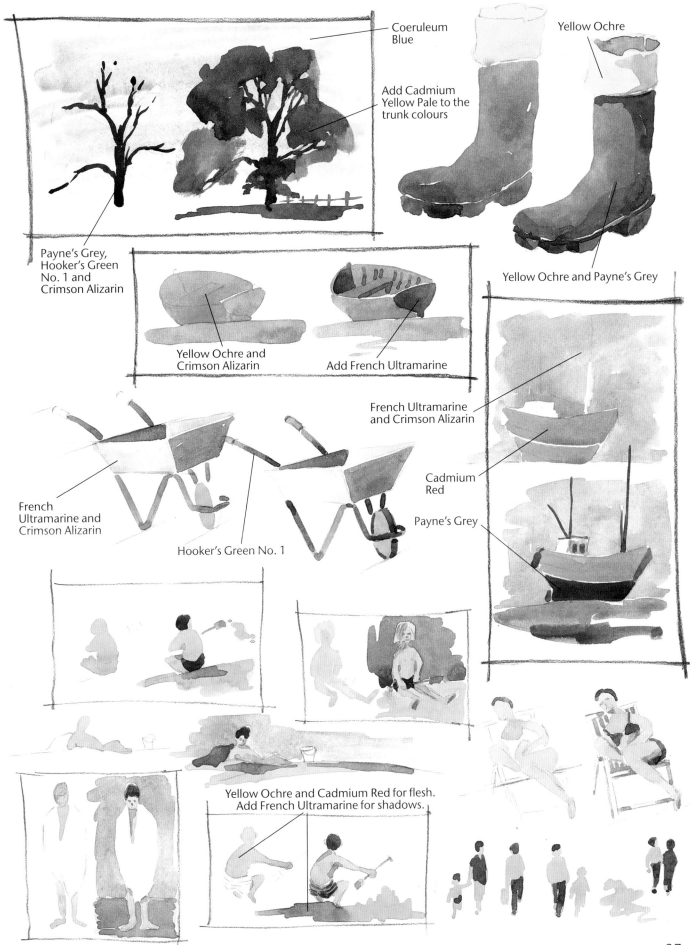

Coeruleum Blue

Add Cadmium Yellow Pale to the trunk colours

Yellow Ochre

Payne's Grey, Hooker's Green No. 1 and Crimson Alizarin

Yellow Ochre and Payne's Grey

Yellow Ochre and Crimson Alizarin

Add French Ultramarine

French Ultramarine and Crimson Alizarin

French Ultramarine and Crimson Alizarin

Cadmium Red

Hooker's Green No. 1

Payne's Grey

Yellow Ochre and Cadmium Red for flesh.
Add French Ultramarine for shadows.

Further exercises

Here are two more simple exercises for you to try. Look at the four stages of my sketch of Sarlat in the Dordogne, France *(below)* and follow them carefully. This sketch was drawn with a 2B pencil on Bockingford watercolour paper, 17 x 15 cm (7 x 6 in). The shadow colour, for the people and inside the archway, is very important to the sketch and was mixed from French Ultramarine, Crimson Alizarin and a touch of Yellow Ochre.

▲ First stage

▲ Second stage

▲ Third stage

▲ Finished stage

▶ I used cartridge paper measuring 15 x 28 cm (6 x 11 in) for this watercolour sketch of Norfolk countryside and started by drawing in the sketch with my 2B pencil. Then I shaded in, using my pencil in the 'long' drawing position (see page 28).

▲ First stage

▶ I painted in the sky with my No. 10 brush and a mix of French Ultramarine and a little Crimson Alizarin. I left the house as unpainted white paper. Then I painted the grass with a mix of Cadmium Yellow Pale and Hooker's Green No. 1 and then used Yellow Ochre, Crimson Alizarin and a little French Ultramarine to put in the path.

▲ Second stage

▶ I made the sky colour darker by adding a little Yellow Ochre and used this to paint in the distant trees. I still left the house as unpainted paper. Then, using the grass colours, but darker, I painted over the trees. Finally, I painted some dark areas on the grass to give form and shape.

▲ Finished stage

Measuring Outdoors

I consider this to be the most important part of sketching. Let us assume that you are ready to start sketching. You must first observe the scene in front of you carefully and become familiar with what you are about to draw. This could take up to 15 minutes, depending on how complicated the subject is and how much time you have to sketch but, believe me, it will be time well spent.

◄ Using a pencil for vertical measuring.

Measuring your subject

At this point you might understand everything you see, but how do you work out the relative sizes and positions of objects in your scene, and transpose them accurately on to your paper?

This is a very important skill to acquire. Although to start with you may find it tedious, or perhaps a little mechanical, you must persevere. It will soon become second nature and as much a part of sketching as putting pencil to paper. The principle is simple. Hold your pencil at arm's length, vertically for vertical measuring and horizontally for horizontal measuring, with your thumb along the near edge as your 'measuring' marker. By always keeping your arm at the same distance from your eye during measuring, the comparative distances will be consistent.

◄ Using a pencil for horizontal measuring.

Finding a key measure

The object of the exercise is to measure the subject and apply it to your paper. Obviously, you do not use the same length to measure your actual subject as you do for the subject on your sketch. You are simply trying to get the correct proportions, so let me take you through the example at the top of the next page.

Suppose the first sketch, **a**, is a real row of houses. Draw a part of your sketch, say house no. 3, on your paper as in **A**. You now need to get houses nos. 1 to 7 on your sketch as they

appear in reality. Hold up your pencil to measure house no. 3 and, as you move your hand along, measure how many widths of house no. 3 will go into the length of the seven houses (nine). Check your sketch, **A**, and using your pencil as a scale, measure whether the width of the house no. 3 you have drawn can be drawn along your paper nine times. In **A** it can be drawn only about five times. So draw a smaller house on the same sketch, **B**, and by simple trial and error you will come to the size of house that will fit on to your paper nine times.

Now hold up the pencil to the real scene to measure how many widths of house no. 3 can be divided into houses nos. 1 and 2. You will find that they are all the same size. Therefore, on your paper, you can measure three houses from left to right, the third being no. 3, which is your key measure, **C**. Looking up at your subject again, measure how many widths of house no. 3 can be divided into house no. 4 (two). On your sketch, using your pencil as a

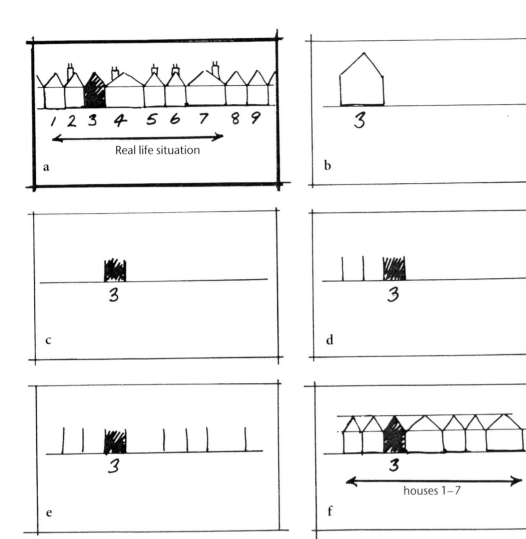

a — Real life situation

1 2 3 4 5 6 7 8 9

b — 3

c — 3

d — 3

e — 3

f — 3 — houses 1–7

◄ How to measure a row of houses and draw them to fit your paper in the correct proportions.

▼ An example of the use of key measures in working out the correct proportions of your sketch. You will see that I used half a key measure here as well.

ruler and your thumb as a marker, measure a distance twice as long as, and to the right of, house no. 3. You thus have the correct measurement for house no. 4. Continue in this way until you have drawn the row of houses from 1 to 7. They will fit your paper exactly, **D**.

Now check the height of the houses. Measure the width of house no. 3 and turn your pencil vertically, with your thumb still in position, to see how many widths of the house will divide into its height. You will find that it fits exactly once, up to the bottom of the eaves. On your sketch, use your no. 3 house measure and mark the height of the houses, as in **E**. Then check the height of the roofs, and so on.

If you take time to do this, you can put as much detail into the houses as you want, knowing that your drawing will end up on your sketchpad (not falling off it!) and it will be proportionally correct.

key measure

A Step-by-Step Sketch

Now that you know how to start a sketch, let's go through the development of a simple one to exactly see how it works. At this stage you have observed your subject, and are sitting or standing comfortably, you know the type of sketch you are going to do, you can measure, and you have decided what your centre of interest is. I shall take you through the stages but look at the finished stage first, to familiarize yourself with the picture.

First stage

The first line to draw is the line of the main field. Position this near the centre of the page then you can add more foreground or sky later. Next position the farm (centre of interest). I wanted this picture to be long and thin, as it was the long line of the farm buildings which inspired me to draw it.

Second stage

Draw the farm buildings in.

Third stage

Complete the buildings. Emphasize the lower part of them so they don't appear to float away. Draw in the hills and the new field.

Fourth stage

Now draw the tree. You will see that I have drawn two more lines across, one above the buildings, and one below. This gives you the long shape of the picture dominated by buildings.

Fifth stage

It is a good idea to add more information if you have the time and this I did in stage 5. The path is extended and the gate and fence have been drawn in. This could make a 'happy', designed picture with the path leading you to the centre of interest.

Finished stage

In the finished stage, I have shown a different picture shape by cutting the sketch off just above the tree. So this one sketch can make three different pictures shapes – stages 4, 5 and 6.

I did this step-by-step sketch with my 2B pencil on tracing paper. The idea was taken from nature, but the sequence of stages was done in my studio to explain, very simply, the progress of a sketch.

▶ So that you can follow the stages, I have developed a simple sketch through from start to finish, and shown how the same scene can be used in three different ways.

▶ **Devon Farm**
2B pencil and watercolour
15 x 25 cm (6 x 10 in)
Try masking this sketch to see how many different pictures you can make.

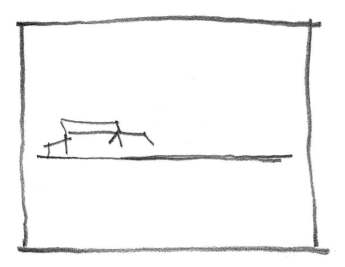

▲ First stage

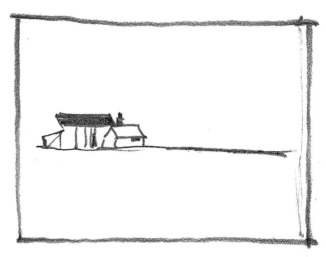

▲ Second stage

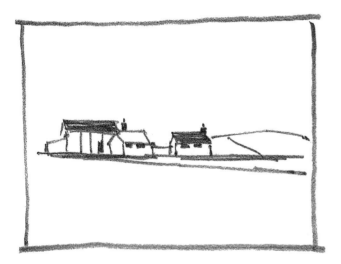

▲ Third stage

▲ Fourth stage

▲ Fifth stage

▲ Finished stage

Sketching Movement

When you are learning to sketch you may think that there are enough complications just sketching something stationary without trying something that moves! As usual, you must observe and understand your subject. If anything, this is even more important for capturing movement. Measuring is also important, but it can be very frustrating; particularly when, for instance, you measure the length of an animal's head to see how many times it goes into the body length, and then it completely changes its position!

When I am asked if I have a magic formula for drawing a moving subject, sadly the answer is no. However, there are ways of approaching your subject that will enable you to master this part of sketching.

Practice and patience

The most important priorities after observation and understanding your subject are practice and patience. Let us assume you are sketching heavy horses. You should look at them and study their most outstanding features. You will find they stand still for minutes at a time. Look for the obvious key

Photographs are a great help when you are sketching moving subjects like animals. Take some to compare with your sketches when you get back home.

▲ **Nigel, the photographer**
2B pencil on cartridge paper
10 x 10 cm (4 x 4 in)

► **Students on one of my courses**
2B pencil on cartridge paper
15 x 14 cm (6 x 5½ in)

44

▲ **Norfolk horses**
2B pencil on cartridge paper
12.5 x 23 cm (5 x 9 in)

positions of their anatomy, such as where a foreleg starts, how long it is compared to the depth of body, and so on. In this way, you are measuring and positioning through observation, before you start to draw.

Learn with your sketches

Your observation could last anything from half an hour to an hour. It's up to you, but don't 'draw with your eyes' for too long or you will find it much more difficult to actually start sketching. When you do begin, carry on at your own speed, observing carefully, and if your subject moves, stop and start another. You may find that your subject regains its original position, or that another horse takes up the same attitude so you can carry on your sketch using a different model!

Never worry that you don't finish one horse completely. You are learning by observing and when you sketch as well, you are recording what you see. This combination of activities will quickly give you a good knowledge of your subject.

▼ **Elephants at Paignton Zoo, Devon**
2B pencil on cartridge paper
23 x 30 cm (9 x 12 in)

Time well spent

Naturally the more you do, the more your sketches will flow. If I were to sketch horses for two hours, I would start by spending about half an hour wandering around looking and observing. The next 10 minutes I would spend sketching. The chances are it would not be very good, but I would be relaxing and getting the 'feel' of the subject. Then, for the next hour, I would work very hard, totally involved in what I was drawing, and that time would be spent gathering useful information. After that, my concentration would start to lapse and the results of the last ten minutes would resemble those of the first ten!

Watching movement on television

One way of training your eye to retain a moving image long enough to draw its shape is to sketch movement on your television screen. This is difficult, but can be done. You won't finish anything and your sketchbook may seem to be filled with unsatisfactory work but these sketches are a means to an end and will train your brain to work and observe faster than normal. You will learn to look for and see things that hadn't occurred to you before, and you will need to see in seconds how to simplify shape and form.

Finally, if you aren't successful in sketching movement, don't worry. Stick to the vast range of stationary subjects – just so long as you enjoy yourself!

▲ This sketch was done on cartridge paper, 25 x 38 cm (10 x 15 in) using my Watercolour Travelling Studio. I did it at an art materials show and my biggest problem was the people who kept blocking my view! But patience prevailed and I was happy with the finished sketch.

When sketching movement, remember my rules – be patient, observe, look for simple shapes and form, work your speed up, and practise, practise and practise!

All the pencil sketches on this page were done in my cartridge sketchbook with a 2B pencil. Both the one with the artist at the easel *(left)* and the group of artists working *(below)* were relatively easy, because everyone stayed in the same position for quite a while. However, the group of people disappearing over the sand dune *(far left)* were there for about one minute! I drew them first, then relaxed and drew the fence and surroundings. The ponies were not quite so fast, but I still had to be quick.

When is a Sketch Finished?

You should stop working on a sketch when you have got the information that you wanted, or when you feel you have been drawing long enough – whether it's because you're tired, hungry, cold or just bored with the subject. Remember, you are sketching to enjoy yourself.

On one occasion I had been sketching for most of the day. I was feeling very tired, and ready to go home, when I saw a group of boats that caught my eye. I decided to do a 'quick' sketch – the last one. (Incidentally there is no such thing as a quick sketch, unless it tells a story.) The result *(shown right)* was disastrous. I still can't make sense of it, even now. It went wrong because I had tried to work fast. There is nothing wrong with that, but my brain was tired and didn't observe so I drew it without 'seeing'. Unless you observe, your drawn lines become meaningless.

▲ This sketch turned out to be a total disaster!

▼ I did this in my A4 cartridge sketchbook as a demonstration for students in Jersey and, as the helicopter came over, I was persuaded to draw it in. I had about 8 seconds to do this!

▲ When I sketched this windmill on cartridge paper, 12.5 x 28 cm (5 x 11 in) with a 3B pencil, it was evening and everything was silhouetted. I have enough information in this sketch to work from at home.

▼ This boatyard sketch was done in my A3 cartridge sketchbook and I certainly had enough information to work from this at home, with the amount of work that I did. It must have been lunchtime, because sadly there were no workmen to draw in. They didn't return until I had finished the sketch!

Some Questions Answered

I decided to present three of my sketches to a group of artists and students so they could question me about them. I haven't included some questions that have been covered in other parts of the book.

Why did you sketch the digger?

I was out sketching one cold February and, as I walked up the road, I saw the mechanical digger. Half of the road had disappeared and there was a massive crater where it had been! I had never seen anything like it and sat down in the middle of the 'road' to record it. It was a typical enjoyment sketch – so unexpected and exciting – and it is now on paper for ever.

What made you position the tower of Windsor Castle in the middle of the picture?

I started with the centre of interest – the tower – and worked on either side of it. (If you are going to paint from the sketch at home, you can decide where you want your centre of interest then.) As it happens I like the composition of the sketch, because the tower and the flag give it a pyramid shape, making the castle look solidly placed on the ground.

What inspired you to do the colour sketch of Sutton Staithe?

The sunlight coming through the trees combined with the warm colour of the building in the background totally inspired me – I just had to sketch it!

How do you scale up a sketch to do a larger picture?

I've drawn a little diagram to show you. Use a ruler and draw a line diagonally across the page from one corner to another. Wherever you draw a line parallel with the top of the sketch page to meet your diagonal line, drop a

perpendicular line down, parallel to the side of your sketch page and that area will be exactly in proportion to your sketch.

How important is sketching?

It teaches you to observe. It takes you out of doors to see and feel nature and to record. It is the life blood of your inspiration. If you can go out sketching – then you should!

▲ The mechanical digger was drawn in my A4 cartridge paper sketchbook with 2B pencil. It is one of the most unusual subjects I have ever sketched!

▼ How to scale your sketch up or down to any size you want while still retaining the correct proportions of your original sketch in your finished painting.

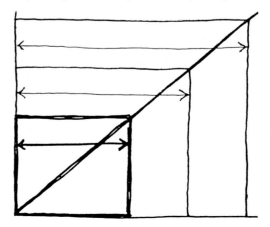

▶ Sutton Staithe, Norfolk
I did this in my A3 sketchbook. I was simply inspired, and what better motive for painting! I enjoyed every minute of this sketch.

▲ Windsor Castle
I used a 2B pencil and drew this in my A3 sketchbook. I have used the sketch to paint from at home, with the aid of a 'very poor' photograph I took at the time.

DEMONSTRATION ONE

Crab Boats

I find this type of sketch very exciting but, with the boats and fishermen continually changing position and the wind blowing your sketchpad, you have to work fast! I was on the beach at Sheringham, Norfolk, when I sketched these crab boats coming in.

Colours

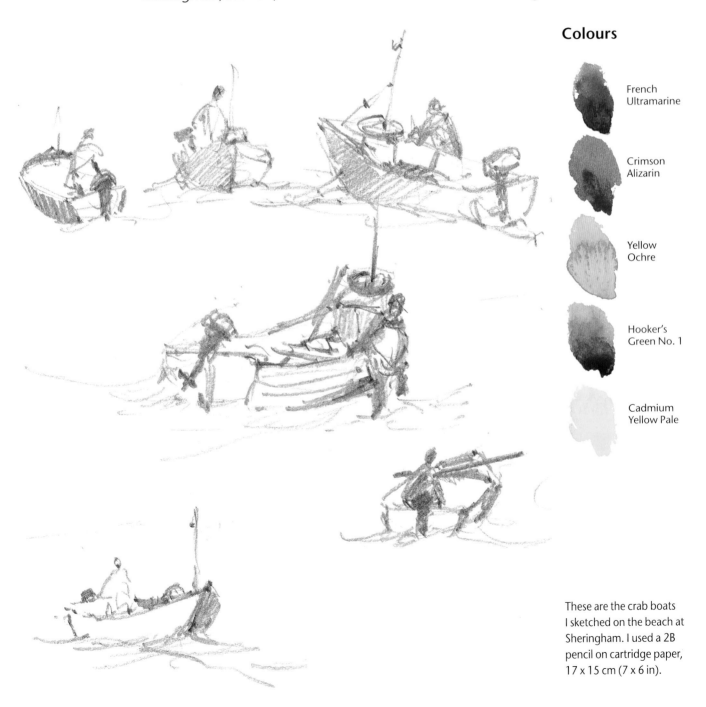

French Ultramarine

Crimson Alizarin

Yellow Ochre

Hooker's Green No. 1

Cadmium Yellow Pale

These are the crab boats I sketched on the beach at Sheringham. I used a 2B pencil on cartridge paper, 17 x 15 cm (7 x 6 in).

First Stage

My references for this sketch were the sketches I did on location (left) and a photograph which I took at the same time. I also had the benefit of valuable 'on the spot' experience.

I tried to recreate the feeling of my location sketches but also added colour. Of course, my studio sketch is a more controlled one than I could achieve sitting on a windy beach!

I started by drawing in the edge of the beach and then put in the main outline of the boat. I drew the two fishermen next and added detail and shading inside the boat. Finally, I drew the boat in the background waiting to come in, the post and the horizon line.

▲ First stage

◄ Detail from first stage, reproduced actual size

▲ Second stage

Second Stage

I painted the sky, working down into the sea with my No. 10 brush and a varying mix of French Ultramarine, Crimson Alizarin, Yellow Ochre and Hooker's Green No. 1 and plenty of water. I left lots of horizontal areas of white paper unpainted to show breaking waves and reflected light. I painted the beach with a stronger mix of Yellow Ochre, Crimson Alizarin and a little French Ultramarine.

In real life, the boat would probably have been pulled up onto the beach by the time you reached the painting stage. This is why it is important to get all your drawing, including any detail needed, done first. After that the boat would still be visible for colour reference and the sky and sea wouldn't have moved!

Finished Stage

I painted the detail inside the boat with my No. 6 brush, using French Ultramarine for the blue trim. Next I painted the dark shadow on the water to the left and the right of the boat and, using the same colour, painted the fisherman's trousers. I added detail to the beach to represent stones, and painted the ramp which the boats are pulled up on and the rope. Then, with Cadmium Yellow Pale and a touch of Crimson Alizarin, I painted the fisherman's yellow waterproofs.

Finally, I added a little colour to the waiting crab boat and put in any darks and detail that I felt helped the sketch.

◄ **Crab Boats, Sheringham**
2B pencil and watercolour on cartridge paper
20 x 30 cm (8 x 12 in)

DEMONSTRATION TWO

Windy Day

This type of sketch works well as a drawing in its own right but if you have time when you are on location it can be fun to add watercolour. I like this way of sketching and do it a lot. This particular spring day was very fresh and blustery. Since I was standing when I did the original sketch, I had to work fast.

First Stage

I positioned the edge of the ploughed field first. Then I put in the right-hand end of the house. I worked to the left, drawing in the roof, chimney stacks and then the big tree, but didn't shade it in case I decided to move its position later – at this stage in a sketch, you can change your mind. I then drew in the small tree on the left and the telegraph pole. Next I drew the house and the trees on the right of the sketch and finally put in the ploughed field furrows.

Once you are happy with the positioning and drawing in your sketch, you can shade in different areas to get your tonal values. The amount of shading you put in on location is entirely up to you.

Second Stage

I used my No. 10 brush and a watery mix of French Ultramarine, Crimson Alizarin and Yellow Ochre for the sky, letting the paint run freely. Then I painted the roof with Cadmium Red and a touch of Cadmium Yellow Pale.

I suggested the distant trees to the left of the house with a mix of French Ultramarine, Crimson Alizarin and a touch of Yellow Ochre. While this was wet, I mixed Hooker's Green No. 1 and Cadmium Yellow Pale and painted into the bottom of the trees, then to the right and over the house. Finally, with the same colour made darker with French Ultramarine and a little Crimson Alizarin, I painted the big tree and the little one to its left with my No. 6 and rigger brushes.

Colours

French Ultramarine

Crimson Alizarin

Yellow Ochre

Cadmium Red

Hooker's Green No. 1

Cadmium Yellow Pale

First stage ▶

▲ Second stage

▼ **Windy Day**
2B pencil and watercolour on cartridge paper
28 x 40 cm (11 x 16 in)

Finished Stage

Using my No. 6 brush, I painted in the distant trees on the right of the house and the small house and bushes. I left the tree trunk as unpainted white paper. Next I painted in the windows and darkened the chimney pots.

The ploughed field was painted with a mix of Crimson Alizarin, Cadmium Yellow Pale and French Ultramarine and I used long brush strokes to represent the furrows. Then I painted over the branches of the big tree, working my brush strokes from left to right to suggest spring leaves blowing in the wind.

You will see that I didn't paint in the right-hand tree. This was for two reasons. Firstly, there was no need, as I could do this when I used the sketch to work from at home. Secondly, I felt it would crowd in on the house and make an archway with the other tree, and I didn't like the composition. If I used the sketch later and decided to paint the second tree, I would make it very pale (sunlit).

DEMONSTRATION THREE

The Beach

This sketch is quite adventurous for beginners to the art of watercolour sketching. A few different compositions could be made from this one sketch, since it covers a very large scene. Have a look at the finished stage and work out different compositions by masking off sections with pieces of paper.

First Stage

I began by positioning and drawing the large block of houses in the top left part of the sketch. Then I positioned the harbour wall. I worked to the left of these houses and then to the right, gradually creating the other houses and cliffs. I didn't put in any tonal shading – I would do this with paint later.

When the 'scene' had been drawn, I drew in the people on the beach. In real life situations, I put people in at the pencil drawing stage, as interesting groups come into my sketching area. Naturally, they are changing all the time, so you must act quickly when you see a group or a person you want to use.

Second Stage

I painted the sky with my No. 10 brush, using a mix of French Ultramarine and a little Crimson Alizarin, and worked down over the distant trees. Then I changed to my No. 6 brush and painted in the red roofs with Cadmium Red and a touch of Cadmium Yellow Pale.

While this was still wet, I painted the 'blue' roofs below with French Ultramarine and a little Crimson Alizarin, letting the two mixes run together in places. Next I painted the side of the red house and then the row of yellow houses, using Yellow Ochre.

Finally, I painted in the roof and windows of the left-hand house.

Colours

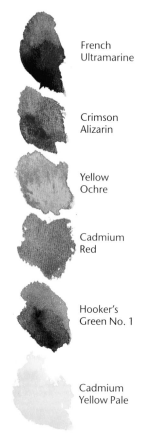

French Ultramarine

Crimson Alizarin

Yellow Ochre

Cadmium Red

Hooker's Green No. 1

Cadmium Yellow Pale

▲ First stage

▲ Second stage

Third Stage

Using my No. 6 brush and a varying mix of Crimson Alizarin and Yellow Ochre for the cliff colour, and Hooker's Green No. 1 and Yellow Ochre for the grass, I started with the cliffs on the left and worked over to the extreme cliffs on the right. I made these paler to give a sense of distance. I kept the paint wet and worked downwards, letting the brush strokes follow the angle of the cliffs. Some unpainted white paper was left showing, which helps to give the impression of the cliffs and their steepness.

Then, with French Ultramarine, a little Crimson Alizarin and Yellow Ochre, I painted in the bridge. When this was dry, I put in the shadows using a darker colour mix.

Once you have painted an area, leave it to dry. Don't keep working over it, or it will become solid and muddy-looking. Try to let the first brush stroke (wash) also be the last – except, of course, when you go over it when it is dry with with a second wash.

▲ Third stage

▶ Detail from third stage, reproduced actual size

Finished Stage

Still using my No. 6 brush, I mixed French Ultramarine, Crimson Alizarin and Yellow Ochre to paint in the sea wall but used less French Ultramarine in the mix for the wall at the end of the beach.

Next I painted in the beach, starting at the top with Cadmium Yellow Pale, then running into Yellow Ochre and Crimson Alizarin, and also French Ultramarine and Crimson Alizarin for the wet parts.

Once the beach was dry, I painted in the flesh colour of the people using Cadmium Red and a touch of Cadmium Yellow Pale. When this was dry, I used bright colours to suggest their clothes, leaving plenty of white paper showing.

Then I painted in some very simple detail on the houses and cliffs, and positioned the trees behind the houses. Finally, I put dark 'blobs' to represent heads on some of the people, and a few shadows.

▲ Detail from finished stage, reproduced actual size

◄ **Dawlish Beach**
Watercolour on Bockingford paper
28 x 38 cm (11 x 15 in)

61

Watercolour Landscapes
By David Bellamy

Watercolour is the most exciting of painting mediums and it often seems to have a mind of its own. It is just as likely to create a gloriously beautiful effect or an unsightly muddy puddle! Whilst it can be thrilling to let the washes get slightly out of control and to hope that the accidental runs will end in a positive result, I shall endeavour to show you how to get the most out of the medium. Hopefully, many of your accidents will end up as happy results.

Like most things, watercolour painting is far easier to cope with when the learning process is broken down into easy stages. If you follow my suggestions, then you should begin to produce competent landscapes very quickly. Many of the rules and ideas that are illustrated here will act as guidelines whilst you are learning, but once your expertise develops, you may wish to discard some of them. I have broken most of the accepted conventions on composition which are outlined in the following pages to good effect on several occasions.

The basic techniques

I aim to teach you the basic techniques of landscape watercolour painting in an organized manner, starting in a simple way

◀ **Waterfall, Cwm Clydach**
30 x 41 cm (11¾ x 16 in)

and then gradually building up to more complicated scenes. Take each section a step at a time, trying out the techniques for yourself.

By practising each technique several times you will become more adept at it; you cannot expect to get all of them right first time. Large pads of cheap cartridge paper are a boon for this type of exercise because you will be less inhibited and be able to paint more freely. When you feel confident, try copying the paintings, starting with the easier ones. Get yourself a dark-coloured rectangular mount to lay over your paintings in order to help you to assess when they are finished.

You will find that many of the chapters overlap. For example, one is dedicated solely to skies, but since most of the paintings I have featured are landscapes you will find instances of skies in them too. So do be sure to look beyond the chapter you are studying to find other relevant examples.

Sketching

This is an important part of working with watercolours but most beginners feel happier possessing a little painting experience before they venture out into the world armed with a sketchbook and pencil.

Whilst it can be daunting at first, going out to work directly from nature is the best thing that a landscape artist can do. I would suggest, therefore, that you become familiar with the basic techniques, copy paintings from the book and then, when you feel ready and in need of fresh material, go out on your own, or with a friend, in search of new subjects. The types of subject that you gravitate towards are important in your development as an artist. We all have certain preferences – mine is wild, untamed scenery – and finding what excites you most is vital as a source of inspiration.

I have covered a wide range of subject matter which is found in the countryside. Once you have tried these subjects you may

▲ Packhorse Bridge, Glen Lyon
26 x 21 cm (10¼ x 8¼ in)

have a much clearer idea of what you wish to concentrate on, but to begin with try to paint as many different subjects as you can.

Drawing

I cannot over-emphasize the importance of drawing – this is especially valid in the case of the landscape artist. Continual practice at pencil drawing will reap rewards. Drawing a still life or scenes from a photograph, and taking every opportunity to draw outside, even if you go no further than your garden, will improve your draughtsmanship.

With practice everyone can improve their drawing skills, and it will certainly have a beneficial effect on your watercolours. Above all, don't become too discouraged if your paintings and drawings are not immediately successful; the more mistakes you make, the faster you will learn!

Watercolour Techniques

Watercolour is a transparent medium. Unlike oils or acrylics you cannot paint lighter colours over a passage of dark paint, so you need to begin with the lightest shades and gradually build up the colour by laying one wash over another. By breaking down the process of producing a watercolour into a number of stages you can make life easier for yourself and, with practice, become freer in expressing a scene.

Laying a flat wash

The first technique you need to learn is how to lay a wash of colour across a piece of paper. Normally this is done during the early moments in the life of a painting, covering large areas such as skies or mountains. For this use a large brush and mix a pool of liquid colour in a saucer or palette well. Make sure it is all liquid and there are no blobs lurking under the surface intent on springing nasty surprises as your brush travels across the paper. Do test the strength of your wash on scrap paper before applying it to a painting.

Position your drawing board at a comfortable angle by placing books or similarly solid items beneath it. This will allow the wash to flow freely down the paper and lessen the likelihood of runbacks forming. These dreadful cabbage-like creatures mysteriously emerge from your washes when water seeps back up into your drying wash.

To lay a wash, charge the brush from the pool of colour and draw it across the surface of the paper, preferably in one movement. Immediately follow on down the paper, slightly overlapping the previous limit with each successive stroke. At the bottom you will most likely find beads of

◀ To lay a flat wash ensure the board is at an angle to enable the colour to flow. Mix a pool of colour and work down the paper, slightly overlapping the previous layer with each stroke. Use a minimum number of strokes.

◀ To lay a graduated wash, that is, a wash that becomes lighter in tone with each new band of colour applied, simply add more water to the brush as you progress with the wash.

liquid forming. Mop these up quickly with a barely damp brush before they spill over or cause runbacks.

Blending colours in a wash

One of the charms of watercolour is in letting the medium have its way, particularly with regard to washes. One effective technique is to blend a dark upper sky into a lighter area below – see the example at the top of page 65. Begin with a very wet wash of weak Cadmium Yellow Pale in the lower half of the sky, then bring it down over the distant hill. Immediately, whilst the wash is still wet, lay a mixture of Cobalt Blue and Cadmium Red over the top part and then bring the wash down until both washes overlap slightly. Sit back and watch the results, and on no account should you

◄ In this example colours are blended together in a wash. Because the hill in the finished painting will be darker than the sky you can happily allow the wash to flow down over the pencil marks. If you tried to stop the wash right on the hill ridge line, an ugly margin would probably appear once you painted in the hill.

interfere with the wash whilst it is drying.

You can improve your skill level by making a number of attempts at each of the techniques that are mentioned here.

Working on wet paper

If you paint into a wet surface, the edges will soften and bleed into the wet area. Unless you deliberately want this effect it can have a disastrous effect on your paintings, but when employed as a technique it can produce exciting soft images. Controlling it, however, can be tricky, so it does take some experience to handle this technique with confidence.

Variegated colours

The first use for dropping further colours into a wet area is to create a pattern of colours, each blending into what has already been laid. This treatment is extremely effective in creating a variegated effect on a wall, depicting the different colours in rock formations, adding interest to a mountain or hillside, creating a patch of moss or lichen on an ancient roof perhaps, or forming a variety of colours in a hedgerow. The possible applications are endless.

The aim of this technique is to add a variety of colour without making it a dominant feature. It is a superb device to use for a monotonous feature, such as a wall, hedgerow or sloping ground, where some detail has been painted in, but too much would overwhelm the eye of the viewer. By substituting excess detail with variation in colour you can create interest in a more subtle way.

This technique works best where the extra colours are dropped into the wet wash immediately, without waiting for it

▼ Various colours were dropped into the original wash of French Ultramarine and Raw Sienna whilst it was still wet. When it was dry some darker shadow areas were introduced on the right. Finally, with a dark mixture of Burnt Sienna and French Ultramarine some of the stones were painted in detail.

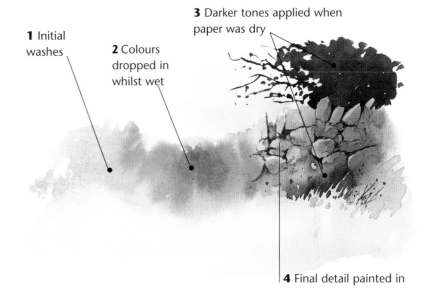

1 Initial washes

2 Colours dropped in whilst wet

3 Darker tones applied when paper was dry

4 Final detail painted in

to start drying. There is less chance of any runbacks forming, unless you deliberately want them. Experiment on scrap paper before you try the technique in a painting. Mop up any excess water with a damp brush.

Wet-into-wet

The main reason for painting on wet paper is to create soft images, such as features barely showing through mist, clouds, reflections in water or distant atmospheric hills. This wet-into-wet technique takes some experience before it can be handled with assurance – the basic problems are knowing when to drop in the second wash and how strong to make the mixture.

For instance, to create soft-edged clouds simply wet the sky area with clean water and then drop in the blue or grey colour which represents the areas in between the white clouds.

Woodland scenes generally benefit from the wet-in-wet technique where the background trees and bushes are rendered whilst the overall wash is still wet. You need to wait until the wash is starting to dry, otherwise the images of background trees

will become lost in the wetness. Make sure that the paint mixture you are about to brush into the wet wash does not hold much water. It needs to be damp with a strong mixture of paint. With a complicated area, do not try to achieve too much in one go – you can always let the paper dry and then re-wet it to have another attempt at the technique.

Creating white spaces

Many watercolourists feel the need to cover every bit of their paper with paint. However, this practice tends to take away the sense of freshness and spontaneity that is the hallmark of a good watercolour. Flecks of white paper here and there are the very soul of a watercolour, bringing it to life.

Because it is difficult to recover a pure white surface once it has been painted over, these white areas are best planned in advance.

Recovering white areas
White areas can be blotted out with tissues whilst the paint is still wet, but the result is dependent on the pigments used: staining

▲ **Lethertor Bridge, Dartmoor**
18 x 21 cm (7 x 8¼ in)
The soft background trees contrast sharply with the hard edges of the clapper bridge, emphasizing the latter as the focal point. The conifers were painted whilst the sky wash was still damp.

pigments, such as Crimson Alizarin or Viridian, are almost impossible to remove from the paper completely.

The sponge is another useful tool for restoring white. Make sure that the paint is dry and then use some clean water and a soft, natural sponge.

Sponging can be effective when used in conjunction with some sort of mask. Two pieces of thin card placed almost together can be held across a dark area of paint which has dried, and the damp sponge drawn up and down along the gap two or three times. By quickly mopping it dry with a tissue, a fine white line appears – a useful technique for creating a white mast. Corners of buildings, light shorelines of lakes and many other applications can be emphasized in this manner.

Masking fluid

By painting masking fluid over the areas you wish to keep white, you can paint over them in watercolour and then rub off the masking fluid when the paint is dry.

Apply the masking fluid with an old brush and immediately wash the brush in warm soapy water, as the masking fluid can harm the hairs. A dip pen can be used for fine detail – see the *Cottage at Kinnersley* demonstration on page 100 for this particular technique.

White paint

White paint, such as Chinese White or White Gouache, can be used in small quantities to suggest white masts, seagulls, flecks of white flowers and many other small features, but when used in large amounts it can detract from a watercolour. The only time when any greater amounts of white paint can be effective is when you wish to paint on tinted paper, where the highlights need to be brought out. If you do use white paint, use it sparingly and apply it at the end of the painting, otherwise any other colours running into it will turn milky.

As a last resort, if you are painting on normal white paper, a knife or scalpel can scratch out a highlight, creating a sense of sparkle, tidying up a distant shoreline or creating a wire fence. It is best not to rely on this technique and only use it if all else fails. Again, wait until everything has been painted before scratching the surface.

Experiment with masking fluid on cartridge paper and try some other techniques for recovering the white of the paper.

▶ **Pembrokeshire Cottages**
20 x 29 cm (8 x 11½ in)
The cottages, and some of the trees, were covered initially with masking fluid – for such fine work you may find a dip pen works well. Strong dark washes accentuate the whiteness.

Colour

With such a large number of colours available it can be confusing trying to work out how to cope with so many. As mentioned in the equipment and materials section, this is best carried out methodically with a limited number of colours. Before going further it is worth looking at the theory behind colour mixing.

Colour theory

You may have already come across terms such as primary and secondary colours, complementary colours and colour temperature. Primary colours are red, yellow and blue. When any two of these are mixed together they produce secondaries: red and yellow produce orange, yellow and blue make green, and blue and red combine to create purple. If a primary colour is

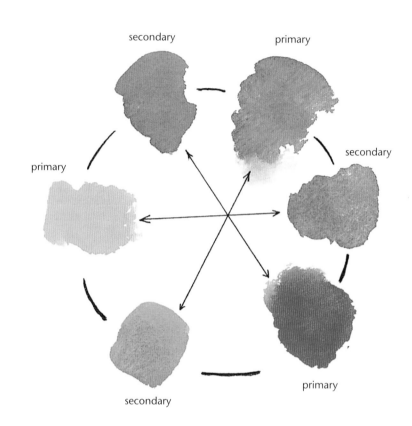

▲ The three primary colours of red, yellow and blue are seen on this simplified colour wheel, with each of their resulting mixtures shown between the appropriate colours. For example, orange appears between red and yellow, and its complementary, blue, is indicated opposite by the arrow.

Cadmium Yellow Deep

Gamboge

Cadmium Yellow Pale

Naples Yellow

Cadmium Red

Crimson Alizarin

Permanent Rose

French Ultramarine

Cobalt Blue

Monestial Blue

◀ Here you can see various shades of yellow, red and blue. The warmest in temperature in each case is positioned to the left. Remember that in a painting, cool colours will recede.

mixed with a secondary colour the result is known as a tertiary colour.

Complementary colours are those found directly opposite each other on the colour wheel, such as blue and orange. If complementaries are placed together they give a more striking impact to a feature. An effective example of this is seen in *Autumn Tints on the Canal* on page 82.

Colour temperature refers to the warmth or coolness of a colour. Whilst reds and yellows tend towards warmth and blues, greens and greys towards the cool, all these colours vary in degree. Permanent Rose, for example, is a cooler red than Cadmium Red. Cool colours will suggest recession, so by using blues and greys for the more distant parts of a scene and warmer colours in the foreground, you can create the illusion of depth in your painting.

Abutting warm and cool colours can suggest warm sunshine or cold snow. For example, a small area of warm-coloured sky can make a landscape covered in snow, which is suggested by cool blues and greys, appear even colder.

Colour mixing

Before you attempt any mixing it is worth looking at some basic considerations regarding colour mixing. Firstly, keep all your colours clean: generous portions of muddy colours taken from the palette will not enhance the freshness of your mixtures. Secondly, it is best to try to achieve the colour you require by mixing only two colours. Sometimes, of course, you do need to use a third, but keep it to a minimum. Using any more colours will simply produce muddy mixtures.

Thirdly, in order to lighten a colour or a colour mixture add water not white paint. White should only be used on its own and not mixed with other colours because it makes them appear milky and opaque. Mixing colours with white will totally lose the fresh and vibrant appeal of watercolour.

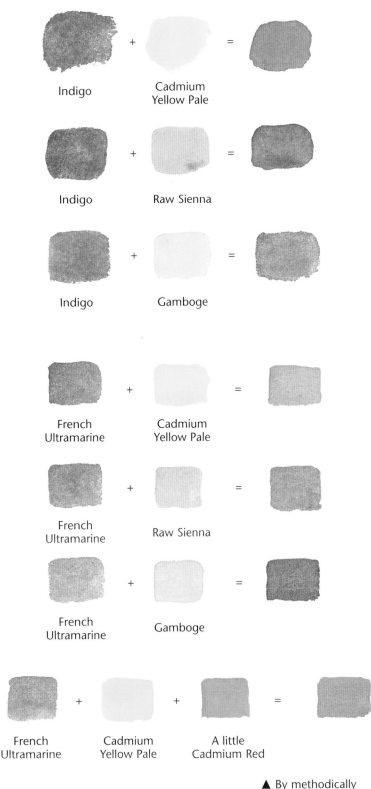

Indigo + Cadmium Yellow Pale =

Indigo + Raw Sienna =

Indigo + Gamboge =

French Ultramarine + Cadmium Yellow Pale =

French Ultramarine + Raw Sienna =

French Ultramarine + Gamboge =

French Ultramarine + Cadmium Yellow Pale + A little Cadmium Red =

▲ By methodically mixing primary colours together you can ascertain which combination produces the green which will best serve your purpose.

69

▼ This diagram illustrates the effect of mixing a number of dark colours with French Ultramarine in order to create a series of four greys, progressing in degrees of warmth from left to right. The colour temperature is most evident in the top sky areas. Try this exercise for yourself. First wash Naples Yellow over the central area – very wet. Then drop in the grey wash above the Naples Yellow and allow the wash to run down into it. Paint the hard-edged background ridge with the same grey in each case, and overlap the dried wash of Naples Yellow. Paint on darker mixes of the same greys when the paint is dry, then soften into Raw Sienna at the bottom.

French Ultramarine + Permanent Sepia   French Ultramarine + Burnt Umber   French Ultramarine + Burnt Sienna   French Ultramarine + Light Red

▶ **Winter at Ponde, Brecknockshire**
21 x 31 cm (8¼ x 12¼ in)
A snow scene benefits from the use of warm colours in places – the sky is an obvious choice. Here, the Raw Sienna on the walls, hedgerows and the chickens helps to counter the stark coldness, further aided by the warm grey of the background trees.

A methodical approach will help you to learn what can be achieved by combining various colours. Take a sheet of cheap cartridge paper – an A4 pad is ideal – and paint a dab of French Ultramarine near the top. To a clean part of your palette or saucer take some more French Ultramarine, wash the brush clean and then add approximately the same amount of Cadmium Yellow Pale. Each time have a generous amount of water on the brush to make the paint flow. Mix the colours well and then apply the mixture as another dab below the French Ultramarine dab. Next, make a similar mix using Raw Sienna and French Ultramarine and continue down the paper, each time noting the colours mixed.

Continuing in this way, you can mix all your colours with French Ultramarine to see what each mixture produces. Of course, if you increase the amount of one colour the resulting mixture will change. Try this experiment several times using a different base colour for each new sheet of paper.

Some colours mix better than others. For example, Naples Yellow is quite opaque and in watercolour painting it is a poor mixer, with the mixture usually resulting in a milky appearance. It is best used on its own because it is excellent for subtly warming up

skies, or for dried grasses. Paints produced by different manufacturers can vary considerably, even colours with the same name, so it is wise to work through your colours methodically to see how they react in various mixes.

It is not necessary to slavishly copy the colours you see in nature. Colour is affected by light – one moment it can appear drab and then suddenly it can come alive when the sun emerges. You may wish to brighten a colour next to the focal point and subdue one in the foreground. Therefore, when you are mixing colours an approximation will suffice in most cases.

▼ Black paint deadens a painting, so to create strong darks use a mixture of colours. In this instance I used French Ultramarine and Burnt Sienna to produce a powerful dark.

Tones

When you start painting in any medium you will become aware of the following terms: tones, tonal values, value. Basically, they all mean the same thing, that is, the degree of darkness or lightness of a colour or feature within a painting. Each colour has its own range of tones. Cadmium Yellow Pale, for example, has a much lower range than Burnt Umber, the latter being so much darker.

Whatever medium you work in, however, the range of tones is very small compared to those that are found in nature. It is impossible, of course, to achieve the brightness of the sun. To a certain extent, therefore, you have to compromise.

At this early stage it is helpful to forget about colours and simply to concentrate on coming to terms with tones. This can be achieved very easily by carrying out a monochrome painting, using perhaps only

▲ These tonal scales demonstrate how many more tonal variations can be achieved with Burnt Umber than with Cadmium Yellow Pale.

some Burnt Umber. *Under the Cotswold Escarpment* has been achieved using this method, but first try the slate fence example that is shown opposite. When you paint a monochrome, work from light to dark as with a normal watercolour.

Get the tone right first time

It takes experience to achieve good results with tones, partly because watercolours tend to lighten in tone as they dry out,

▶ **Under the Cotswold Escarpment**
12 x 15 cm (4¾ x 6 in)
This was painted using only Burnt Umber. Using a dark colour to paint a monochrome will help your progress as you do not need to concern yourself with colour selection. This allows you to concentrate on tones.

some pigments more so than others. Payne's Grey can be wayward in this respect, ending up far lighter than when it is applied.

It is important to try and get the tone right first time and not to take the attitude that 'I can always lay a darker wash on top if this one ends up too light'. Inevitably, it *will* end up lighter and another wash will be required, sometimes even more. After a number of gradually increasing darker washes you will almost certainly end up with a muddy colour!

Avoiding the linear look

One of the most important lessons to learn is that although you may be used to drawing with a pencil or pen, which are linear tools, it is tone that defines the features within a painting, not line. In nature, the edges stand out not because Mother Nature has drawn convenient lines around each object, but because the light is creating different tones according to whether the object is reflecting or absorbing light, the various angles and the local colour. A red roof against a dark green mass of trees may look obvious when seen 25 cm (10 in) away as you paint it, but from 2 m (79 in) or more it can become lost if the

tones are the same, even with two completely different colours.

Light does play tricks on us, changing tones as the various elements are caught in sunlight and shadow – an up-turned black-tarred Irish curragh lying near the beach can be the lightest part of a scene if it is caught glinting in sunlight. Therefore, you do have to modify tones and colours according to the light effects. Once you begin to make effective use of tones, you are well on your way to producing good watercolours.

▲ Grey slate fences are peculiar to Snowdonia, and this watercolour sketch depicts one against a variety of grey backgrounds. The tones are increasing in strength towards the right, making the right-hand side of the fence appear closer.

▶ This rough pencil sketch illustrates clearly how using tones to define objects gives a more natural appearance than relying solely on pencil lines.

◀ **Bow Fell, Lake District**
19 x 34 cm (7½ x 13½ in) Because there is little colour in this painting, it relies primarily on tonal variation for its strength. In a scene like this, it is important to compare the foreground dark tones with those on the mountain to achieve a sense of recession.

Composition

Composition relates to the way in which you build up a painting – where you put each feature, how much emphasis you give it, how big, how small and how each item relates to its neighbour.

When considering the composition, you need to ask yourself several questions. Do you want to emphasize peace and tranquillity, or perhaps dynamism and drama? Is a vertical – portrait-style – format best, or a horizontal one? Perhaps an elongated view would yield optimum results. For peace and tranquillity the horizontals should dominate, whilst drama is suggested more by verticals.

Just as it is useful to jot down notes before writing an essay or a report, it can help enormously to commit your ideas to paper before beginning a painting. For this, studio sketches are critical.

The studio sketch

Once you have mastered the compositions suggested here, you can try working from your own sketches or photographs.

When you are doing your painting from photographs, it is helpful in most cases to produce a studio sketch to ascertain the focal point, how it needs to be emphasized, whether there are supporting elements, what can be added or omitted, how high to place any mountains, trees, cottages, and so on. At this point, you can also consider the main tones and how each feature will relate tonally to its neighbour.

Studio sketches can also be useful if your original sketch is complicated or you are working from more than one sketch or photograph. This can happen, for example, if you wish to include animals or figures that did not appear in the original scene.

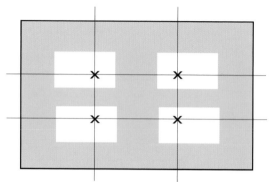

◀ The optimum position for the focal point is roughly one-third from two of the four edges of a painting, as marked by the crosses. The areas marked in green are not suitable for a focal point.

When you are happy with your design, you can transfer it to watercolour paper.

The centre of interest

Composition is discussed extensively throughout this section of the book, but here it is beneficial to consider some general points. Most importantly, however beautiful a scene may be, without a focal point it is unlikely to appeal as a painting. Where this centre of interest is placed is of great importance – study how this has been done in the paintings in this book.

▲ **Barn in the Black Mountains**
18 x 25 cm (7 x 10 in)
The focal point in this scene is the barn. The road, dark ridge descending from the right and the left-hand hedgerow help to emphasize its importance. Bright, warm colours and strong tonal contrasts also help to accentuate the focal point.

◀ These diagrams show you some of the more common composition problems and give you an idea of how they can be improved. In each case, the right-hand diagram offers an improved format.
a: The cottage is too central and the path leads away from it. By moving the gate up to the cottage, the path can lead directly to the building. A bush on the right helps to balance the composition.
b: A fence, hedgerow, wall or other obstruction across the foreground will inhibit the eye of the viewer resting on the centre of interest. Keep your foregrounds simple.
c: Here there are too many competing features. By subduing or eliminating some buildings, the main cottage stands out as the focal point.
d: Sometimes it is difficult to pick out a centre of interest in a scene. Here, one tree has been emphasized by making it stronger in tone in comparison with the others. The sky and lighting also help to highlight it.

Sometimes you will need to reinforce a feature in a particular painting by making it much more prominent and also by supporting it with some other items. Light, shadow and tonal contrasts are powerful ingredients in this respect.

There are times when you need to create a centre of interest by, for example, adding a figure or animal in the most effective position. Lines, such as mountain ridges, harbour chains, hedgerows and fences, can accentuate the importance of the focal point if they lead the eye towards it – roads, tracks and rivers are especially powerful in this respect. This lead-in can often make or break a composition.

Creating Recession

Trying to create a three-dimensional scene on a two-dimensional surface is not an easy task for the artist. A landscape painting needs to suggest a sense of depth and space, whether it is a wide panorama or a more intimate view.

In order to achieve this, you need to adopt a number of techniques. In a scene of distant hills, for example, which has a great sense of spaciousness, you can see that, with a little observation, atmosphere, in the form of mist, heat haze, snowfall or rain, will modify how you observe the more distant objects. Objects seen far away tend to become more blue-grey as they recede, and also to lose detail.

With a more intimate subject, such as a woodland scene, a bend in the river or perhaps a farmyard, you would normally have to emphasize or even create a sense of depth, so that objects stand out. In effect,

you are compressing the space element. This approach not only suggests distance, but helps to avoid too much clutter by reducing the amount of detail.

Emphasizing recession

There are four basic elements that affect the sense of recession: colour temperature, tone, detail and the relative size of objects. Cool colours, such as blues or greys, emphasize a sense of distance, whilst warmer colours, such as reds and most yellows, come forward. Darker tones appear to be closer because objects tend to lighten in tone as they become more distant. Detail acts in the same way.

Colour temperature and tone, however, can work both ways. In a scene where the distance is warmer than the foreground you will need to counter this with strong tones

▶ **Nedd Fechan River, South Wales**
14 x 18 cm (5½ x 7 in)
In more intimate scenes, where the detail is compressed into a smaller area, you normally have to emphasize the feeling of depth by exaggerating the atmosphere. In the actual subject there was barely any tonal difference between the closest and furthest trees as they were not far apart. By creating a strong sense of misty atmosphere the painting retains an appearance of depth.

▶ **Brentor, Dartmoor**
24 x 33 cm (9½ x 13 in)
Brentor is barely visible, a cool and featureless blue-grey colour, whilst the ridges below it are slightly warmer and stronger in tone. This creates a sense of recession, with the strongest tones and detail on the trees and foreground further contributing to the sense of spaciousness. The surface texture of the paper – Waterford Rough – helps to suggest the ragged cloud edges and dry-brush effect below the gate.

▲ Lindisfarne, Northumberland
10 x 17 cm (4 x 6¾ in)
In this painting, a cool background and warm foreground help to suggest depth.

and detail in the foreground. If there are powerful darks in the distance, such as a cloud-covered mountain, for example, then warmer foreground colours and detail will effectively retain a sense of recession. Familiar objects, such as trees, houses, animals, fenceposts and so on, will appear smaller in the distance. You can easily check these points out for yourself, choosing a variety of different atmospheric days to look at the landscape.

When you have identified the focal point, you must consider how your treatment of it will affect the sense of recession. If the focal point is in the middle distance, or further away, you still need to give it appropriate emphasis in terms of strong tonal contrast and perhaps bright colours, but this will need to be countered by stronger tones or detail in the foreground.

Simple Perspective

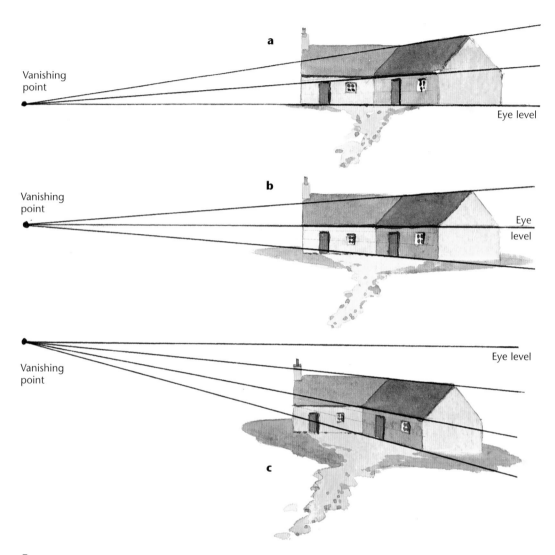

a

Vanishing
point

Eye level

b

Vanishing
point

Eye
level

Eye level

Vanishing
point

c

◄ These views show
how perspective is
altered at three different
eye levels. At **a** the eye
level is at floor height,
so you are looking up at
the house. Note that
the higher you look
above the eye level, the
greater the angle of
the line that extends to
the vanishing point. At
b the line of the eaves is
at eye level. At **c** you
are high above the
building looking down,
which accentuates the
angles of the right-hand
section even more than
in **b**. In each case, the
left-hand part of the
building has remained
more or less the same
as it is directly in front
of you and its horizontal
lines are running
parallel with your
horizon – a useful point
if you want to make life
easy for yourself!

Linear perspective does not play a major
part in landscape painting, and where it
does impinge on the composition, you can
effectively reduce its impact. Nevertheless, it
is prudent to have a basic understanding of
how perspective affects the objects you wish
to include in a painting.

Buildings

Buildings, especially those that are in close
proximity to one another, tend to present
the most obvious perspective problems. By

pushing them further back into your
composition, they will become easier to
render, mainly because the acute angles are
simplified. There is a natural tendency to
draw or paint buildings that are too large,
so it is worth studying the paintings in this
book that include buildings – you will see
that the majority are quite small in relation
to the size of the painting.

Perspective problems can be exacerbated
further by trying to draw ancient structures
that sag or lean to one side, making the
perspective look incorrect even before you

begin. I usually exaggerate this type of effect because it tends to add character and also to make the effect so obvious that the viewer realizes the building is intentionally wayward.

It is, of course, the horizontal lines that create difficulties, since all vertical lines should remain vertical. When a building is some distance away it is not easy to see much variation in the horizontal lines, and in these cases it usually helps to draw these lines as if they were horizontal, even if they vary slightly in angle.

If you are working with the subject in front of you, then holding a pencil horizontally in front of your eye helps you to judge how true the main lines are. It cannot be a perfect guide, but it is usually adequate. If the building is a considerable distance above or below your eye level, you will get some distortion, especially if you are observing at some distance to one side of the building.

Shorelines

The shorelines of lakes and rivers can, at times, induce strange effects and, if you are not careful, your paintings can make the

▶ Many students emphasize the curves of the shoreline of a lake and so give a sense of looking down from a great height, as in **a**, when in fact they are standing beside the bank. By flattening out the shorelines, as in **b**, the final image is much more pleasing.

water look as though it is flowing over the edges and onto the banks. To create a pleasing composition of a large expanse of water, you have to resort to certain artificial devices at times in order to make the whole scene look authentic. Take care when rendering the banks and adjacent features.

Creating minor intermediate promontories is a device that can enhance a shoreline lacking in interest and it can also improve the perspective, as shown in the lake studies above.

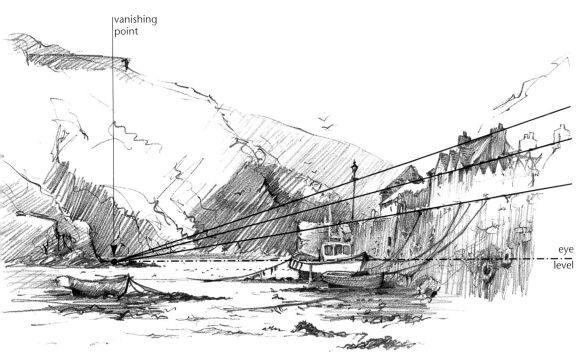

◀ **Fishguard Harbour, Pembrokeshire**
17 x 29 cm (6¾ x 11½ in)
The perspective in harbours can be very difficult. Establish your eye level by using a pencil held horizontally at arms length and closing one eye. It won't be precise, but it will give you an idea of where things fit. Note that, the higher or lower the lines are from your eye level, the more acute the angle to the vanishing point.

Painting Trees

Trees form such an important part of the landscape that it is worth devoting time and effort to learn how to paint them. A lovely river scene, for example, will be spoilt by a backdrop of trees that look like sticks of semi-shredded celery. Trees can be the centre of interest, a supporting feature or they can simply be included for pictorial balance.

Each season holds its interest. Generally I prefer the winter tree, since the lovely shapes of the branches are shown to advantage and other features, such as farms and bridges, are not obscured by masses of foliage.

Trees as a focal point

Generally, you will find that a tree becomes a centre of interest either because it is a prominent specimen and attracts the eye – almost as a picture in itself – or because you are confronted by a beautiful scene which is composed of many trees but has no real outstanding focal point.

In the latter case, it makes sense to select the most handsome example amongst the trees and to emphasize it more than the others. This can be achieved by making it larger than its neighbours, introducing stronger detail or some splashes of brighter

colours – I sometimes drop in a strong red into a tree wash to give it a boost, even if it is not present. You can even accentuate the light and shadows.

When incorporating trees as a focal point you have considerable latitude in deciding which ones to include, omit, or move around, unlike a farm or village scene, since many painters feel it is not cheating to move a tree or two. A prominent gateway, section of fence, or perhaps an animal next to the tree can support it effectively. You could even add a puddle for good measure.

Summer foliage

The mass of summer greenery, especially where there are many trees, can be overwhelming for the artist. If you include more than three or four greens, the painting can start taking on the appearance of patchwork, so resist the urge to paint every shade of green you can see. A yellow or red tinge added to a green mass, can, even in summer, improve matters and the copper beech can be a real saviour!

Foliage attracts many shadow areas, which may look fine in reality or in a photograph but can be disastrous in a painting. I normally resolve this problem by greatly

▼The tree is a good subject to use as a focal point. In **a** the subject appeared rather dull. Therefore, in **b,** a brighter yellow was used to give more impact and a gate added for support. The introduction of animals would have helped further.

a

b

reducing the number of shadow areas and unifying those that are included. I do this by placing the shadows on the side away from the light source and adding some shadow beneath the bulk of the foliage mass.

The best time to observe this effect is in the early morning or late evening when the sun is low, and creating this larger and less fragmented shadow mass will greatly enhance your summer trees. Remember to add the cast shadow of the tree and include the effects of other features in close proximity, as even on the dullest of days there is a darker area beneath a summer tree. Autumn trees are handled in much the same way, but use warmer colours and perhaps show more branches.

Winter trees

Here you can accentuate the beauty of the trunk and branches. Are they angular or swept by graceful curves? If the tree is to be close to the foreground, consider the bark

textures and colours, and perhaps how the shadows cast by the branches fall across the trunk. Work outwards from the tree centre with your brushstrokes, working towards the extremities of the branches. A No. 1 rigger is excellent for fine branch work, but you will need a larger brush for the trunk and thicker branches.

I enjoy using rough paper in a situation like this because it accentuates the bark texture. It also helps enormously when using the scrubbing technique, which, when

▲ **Summer Beeches**
15 x 21 cm (6 x 8¼ in)
Try to avoid having too many different greens in a painting. Here, I added a little Cadmium Orange in places whilst the green was still wet. I used Bockingford Rough paper to emphasize the foreground sparkle and trunk textures.

◄ **House in the Yorkshire Dales**
21 x 28 cm (8¼ x 11 in)
Even when you cannot see any trunks or branches in the summer foliage, it is worth adding in a few to give the tree a sense of form. Always bear in mind the direction of the light.

brushing paint with the side of the brush, creates the illusion of a mass of branches. This will automatically create natural gaps in the paint caused by the rough surface. In a foreground tree, try to give it the appearance of depth by making the branches furthest away from you slightly weaker in tone and bringing forward some branches across the trunk. When painting a late autumn scene, a few warm-coloured leaves scattered in places helps to add a sense of time.

Woodlands and massed trees

Painting woodland scenes can be extremely difficult, so try to simplify the scene by omitting a lot of trees. A misty background with a few trunks rendered with the wet-in-wet technique can be highly effective in a painting. Resist the temptation to add more trees. The painting will benefit from a lead-in, such as a footpath, track or a stream, which winds out of sight around a prominent tree that acts as the focal point. So many woodland paintings are spoilt by

giving equal prominence to many trees.

When you are painting massed trees carefully consider where the mass will end and give the end two or three trees more detail than the others. The painting *Morning Sunlight on the Sussex Downs* on page 90 shows this technique clearly. Broad washes with a hint of tree shapes blending in here and there are more effective than trying to paint every tree you can see.

Choose a few of the more prominent examples within the mass of trees and paint these with their lower trunks and detail softened off into a misty mass. Don't feel that you have to cover every square centimetre of the paper with tree detail!

◄ Autumn Tints on the Canal
27 x 21 cm (10½ x 8¼ in)
Strong sunlight produces cast shadows across the towpath and highlights the left-hand sides of the three main trees on the right bank. Note how the sunlit edges are harder, whilst the shadow sides are generally softer. In each case, the foliage colours were applied first and then, when the paint was completely dry, given shape by defining the shadow areas.

▼ Lane with Birches
21 x 18 cm (8¼ x 7 in)
Light catching the white on the birch trunks was rendered by using masking fluid. When it was removed, the texture on the trunks was painted in.

Painting Skies

Skies can set the mood of a landscape painting, so it is important to plan your sky before wielding your brush across the paper. The sky present in the actual scene rarely helps the composition, so you often have to resort to changing the sky or enhancing it to complement the landscape. This is especially true if you are working from photographs, since they often bleach out the sky detail. Additionally, the cloud formations can be used to balance a composition, accentuate a focal point or simply act as a backdrop.

If the area of sky is small relative to the overall size of the picture, then a simple sky tends to work best. Large loose washes painted with a mop brush best illustrate areas of blanket cloud or blue sky without any detail. A useful technique is to begin with a light wash of weak Cadmium Yellow Pale or Naples Yellow painted horizontally across the lower sky, and then to

immediately drop in the darker cloud bank above it, allowing it to run down into the yellow and creating a lovely loose wash. This will give watercolour its way, encouraging a loose and spontaneous effect.

Integrating sky and ground

Where you have most of the ground detail on one side of a painting then balance can be created by strengthening the cloud formations on the other side. Always consider the sky at the same time as the main composition.

If you wish to emphasize the focal point, direct the most prominent cloud shapes around the area above it, or perhaps create shafts of light leading towards the focal point – this will effectively strengthen the composition. It works particularly well with a hill-top castle, a crag or tree that rises above the main horizontals. This integration

► Practise wet-into-wet cloud studies on scrap paper or the backs of failed watercolours. Try dabbing out with tissues and dropping in strong mixtures of colour at various stages of drying.

▲ Sunset, River Cleddau, Pembrokeshire
20 x 32 cm (8 x 12½ in)
Having the lightest part of the sky filtering through trees creates a powerful image. Here Cadmium Yellow Pale was washed over the area where the trees would appear and then blended into a mixture of Cobalt Blue and Crimson Alizarin further down. When the first application was dry, I laid on a stronger mixture of the same colours to create the warmth of the afterglow of a sunset.

▶ Essex Farm

21 x 32 cm (8¼ x 12½ in)
One of the simplest, yet most effective, skies can be achieved by wetting the whole sky area and then laying on a weak yellow wash in the lower part. In this case I used Naples Yellow. Immediately drop in a stronger pre-mixed wash – here it was French Ultramarine and Burnt Umber – right across the top of the sky, perhaps bringing it down further on one side. Don't forget to keep your board at an angle.

of sky and landscape features adds a powerful sense of authenticity to your work.

It is important to get the transition between sky and ground correct. So many paintings are spoilt by the artist bringing the sky wash down just as far as the distant hills and then stopping abruptly, letting the paint dry and then laying another wash for the hill, trying desperately to abut sky and hill without creating an ugly margin. This is extremely difficult, so bring the sky wash down over the area where the hill will appear, then paint the hill over it once the sky is dry.

If, however, you want a lighter hill, you will need to paint the hill first and then bring down the darker sky over the hill. This can add considerable interest, without over-emphasizing the point, where you wish to introduce counterchange across a background hill or mountain. Having the sky darker than the mountain on one side and lighter on the other can create interest in a subtle manner.

With many monotonous whaleback ridges I often bring in some mist on one side to avoid the ridgeline extending all the way across the painting. This technique is especially striking in the painting of *Tigh Geal, North Uist* on page 115.

Try some exercises on cloud studies based on the illustrations in this section and other parts of the book, ignoring the ground detail to begin with. Later on you can integrate sky and land.

Multi-stage skies

In order to create more interesting skies, a two-stage or three-stage sky can add more depth. Beware of overworking, however. Whilst you can sometimes get away with an overworked foreground, an overworked or muddied sky will ruin your painting. First, you will need to work out where the most prominent and important clouds will appear in your painting. Will they be highlighted dark against light or vice versa? Again, counterchange on cloud formations can be very effective.

It is vital to ensure that the direction of light is constant, and generally most of the time you will find that the hard edges of clouds appear towards the sun. Avoid having hard edges all round the cloud by

▶ **Farm in Arkengarthdale, Yorkshire**
20 x 30 cm (8 x 11¾ in)
The crisp edges of white clouds can only be achieved on dry paper. Here, I began with a wash of Cobalt Blue over the upper sky, immediately adding in some Permanent Rose into the central 'V' and the right-hand side of the paper. When this was dry, I added a mixture of Cobalt Blue and Permanent Rose to suggest harder edged clouds in the centre, then Cobalt Blue and Raw Sienna into other areas of cloud.

◀ **Misty Mountain**
18 x 28 cm (7 x 11 in)
Use the sky effects to complement ground features. In this sketch I painted the sky first, then the crag. Whilst the crag was still wet I brushed the ridge up into the sky area to suggest mist coming down towards the crag. Alternatively, I could have waited for it to dry and then gently sponged the ridge to give a mist-like impression.

softening them off with a damp brush in places, otherwise they can look like a galaxy of deformed balloons. For those you wish to appear wind-torn, apply the wash with the brush on its side. This can be accentuated further by using rough paper rather than Not. The technique of dropping further colours into wet clouds can work extremely well – for example, where you wish to suggest a shadow beneath a cloud.

▶ **Herefordshire Barn**
18 x 27 cm (7 x 10½ in)
This sky was achieved by completely wetting the paper first and then dropping in a strong application of Cobalt Blue to create the white soft-edged clouds. Lower down I brought in some Naples Yellow whilst the paper was still wet. I then added a few darker clouds with a mixture of Cobalt Blue and Cadmium Red.

DEMONSTRATION FOUR

Vallay Strand

By moving away from the subject you can often reduce it to basic shapes and create a much more simplified composition. Whilst this is particularly important when learning to paint, it also has the advantage of giving more impact. There is a wonderful sense of spaciousness in the Hebrides, an aspect that was a prominent ingredient in this demonstration.

◀ First stage

Colours

 Coeruleum Blue

 Naples Yellow

 French Ultramarine

 Cadmium Red

 Raw Sienna

 Light Red

 Burnt Sienna

First Stage

For this demonstration I chose Waterford Not 300 gsm (140 lb). The drawing was first outlined using a 3B pencil. I then laid a wash of Coeruleum Blue over the sky with a large squirrel-hair mop brush, leaving white patches here and there. Whilst this was still wet I brushed some weak Naples Yellow into the lower part of the sky down to sea level. The mountain was darker in tone than the sky so it was unnecessary to stop the yellow wash at the top of the mountain ridge.

Second Stage

Once the washes were dry, I painted the large dark cloud on the right-hand side using a mixture of French Ultramarine and Cadmium Red, again bringing the paint down over the mountain area. Immediately, I brought in some Raw Sienna below the cloud, allowing the two colours to run into one another. The left-hand cloud was then added and the bottom was softened with a damp brush.

After dragging weak French Ultramarine horizontally across the bay, allowing white to shine through in places, I dropped in the mixture of French Ultramarine and Cadmium Red into the sea beneath the left-hand cloud to suggest a reflection.

Once all the washes were dry I took up a No. 10 round sable to paint the mountain with a slightly stronger version of the wash used for the dark cloud, blending it down into the Raw Sienna on the right. By keeping to a few colours the work is given much greater unity. Again, I waited for this wash to dry before rendering the buildings and the ridge on which they stood with a mixture of French Ultramarine and Light Red.

At this three-quarters stage in a painting it is a good idea to stand away from the painting to see how it is developing – this will also help you to assess whether your tones are correct.

Finished Stage

Using a fine-pointed No. 4 round brush loaded with a strong mix of French Ultramarine and Light Red, I suggested some detail on the houses and dark rocks in the water. Stronger Raw Sienna was then dragged across the foreground ground, with some Light Red dropped in in places. The darker sea foreground was achieved with French Ultramarine, Raw Sienna and a touch of Cadmium Red. Finally the foreground rocks were painted in, and the finest detail and birds were added using a No. 1 rigger loaded with Burnt Sienna and French Ultramarine.

▲ Second stage

▼ **Vallay Strand, North Uist**
22 x 34 cm (8¾ x 13½ in)

Painting Water

Water can breathe life and sparkle into a painting, whether it is a tumbling mountain stream, a placid lake, a waterfall, a weed-strewn canal or crashing surf. Even the humble muddy puddle can transform an otherwise dull watercolour painting.

To the beginner, tackling water can appear complicated. However, if you begin with its easier forms, progress should soon be made. As with so many techniques in watercolour, it helps to preserve one's sanity by practising on a scrap of paper rather than trying it out in the foreground of an almost-complete watercolour.

The puddle

A foreground will often benefit from the addition of a puddle because it can break up an otherwise monotonous area or act as a lead-in towards the focal point. Take care when positioning the water, since it usually works best where a feature, such as a gatepost, can be reflected in it.

Strong tonal contrast between water and the surrounding ground accentuates the puddle. Sharp edges will create the same effect although, in places, it can be particularly effective to lose the edge in an indefinite area to create variety and to suggest watery mud.

Breaking up edges with grasses, reeds, boulders and similar features can also vary the interest in the puddle. Counterchange works exceptionally well here, where you can render a dark area of water against light ground on one side, changing the other side to light water against dark mud. Lumps of mud and earth also add interest to the edge of a puddle.

▶ **Morning Sunlight on the Sussex Downs**
23 x 33 cm (9 x 13 in)
Puddles can bring life to the foreground or middle distance and strong contrasts between water and ground are vital. Observe the left-hand puddle and see how the dark water on the far side describes the edge, whilst the grass bank and dark mud are rendered against the lighter part of the water. Having one or two points where the edge is indefinite helps to relieve the hard edges.

Reflections

I use two methods for creating reflections. The first is wet-into-wet, where I drop the reflecting shape into a wet area. Sometimes, the edges of the reflection need to be tidied up with a damp brush, as the paint may stray outside the area that should contain the reflection. The second method involves painting the reflected object upside down, allowing it to dry and then glazing over the area with a weak wash. This is usually blue-grey, but sometimes I add other colours to hint at reflected colours.

This second method automatically subdues the colour and tone in the reflection, but with the first method you do need to make sure that the reflection is not the same intensity as the actual object that is being reflected.

Alternatively, you can put in the reflections on to dry paper, but you need to be very accurate with your tones. I find that this technique does not work as well as the first two. It is worth breaking up reflections with one or two horizontal light slivers – these can be pulled out with a damp half-inch flat brush used on its edge. This works especially well on dark reflections but, because it can be highly effective, do resist the temptation to cover the whole foreground with silver streaks!

▲ **Loch a' Chroisg, Northern Highlands**
24 x 35 cm (9½ x 13¾ in)
I laid a weak wash of Cobalt Blue with a bit of Cadmium Red across the loch. Cadmium Yellow Pale was dropped into the central area to reflect the colour to the right of the dark trees. The reflections of those trees were rendered into the wet loch area with a mix of French Ultramarine and Raw Sienna.

Moving water

If it is kept simple, then moving water can be easier to paint than still water with complicated reflections. The dry-brush technique is extremely effective in rendering sparkling, moving water, especially when it is used in conjunction with rough paper.

With this technique, use a large round brush charged with paint but only a small amount of water. Hold the brush at a low angle over the area to be covered and rapidly drag the brush across the paper. It is worth testing that you have the right consistency of paint on the brush by trying it out on the margin of the paper beforehand. After laying it on, soften any hard edges and allow the paint to dry. Later

you can paint adjacent darker areas of water, rocks or vegetation.

To create water tumbling over rocks, brush the paint on in the direction of the flow of the water movement, as with any turbulent water, but leave a few speckles of white paper showing in places. This gives a great sense of sparkle and liveliness. Reflected colour can be dropped into the wet area if it is significant.

Waterfalls

Here again, strong contrasts between falling water and the adjacent banks and rocks will help to give a sense of falling water. Soft-edged cascades of water that are set against hard-edged dark rocks work best if they are kept simple. Avoid trying to include every

▼ **High Sweden Bridge, Lake District** 22 x 28 cm (8¾ x 11 in) Directly beneath the bridge the water is calm and wet-into-wet reflections have been dropped in – you often have to control these with a damp brush to make sure they don't spread too much. Lower down, white patches have been retained amongst the dabs of French Ultramarine and Burnt Umber. Note how, even on a rain-swept day, the tops of the rocks are catching the light quite strongly.

nuance of tone within the falling water, especially those intrusive vertical strokes that are so easy to overwork. Where the water falls in front of the rocks, keep the edge as soft as possible.

Rough paper can be useful to achieve the ragged edges of cascading water. Observe how the aerated water at the point where the falling water hits the pool below is generally the lightest part. Don't feel that you have to put every rock into the composition. Watch for any light reflection of the falling water in the pool.

Water can be tricky to paint, even for the experienced artist. However, if you keep your washes really fluid you will find that your work gradually improves. Remember to look for any colours that might be present in the reflections and then drop them in straight away.

▲ Ogwen Falls, Snowdonia
20 x 17 cm (8 x 6¾ in)
When painting waterfalls, it is critical to observe the contrasts between tumbling white water and dark rock, and the softness of the water against the hard edges of the rocks. Try not to include every nuance of tone in the water as it is so easy to lose the freshness. Note how the undersides of the rocks soften into the water, with hard edges visible where the rocks come in front of the water.

Try some of the following techniques: the dry-brush method, lifting off a sliver of paint from a dark wet wash with the edge of a half-inch flat brush, and try scratching effects using a scalpel. Paint a series of puddles with a variety of reflections.

▲ Dornoch Firth
10 x 22 cm (4 x 8¾ in)
During a wild moment I accidentally brought the brush down too far when rendering the centre part of the far shoreline. By waiting for the paint to dry completely, I was then able to scrape away the offending colour with a scalpel and to restore the shoreline to the horizontal.

DEMONSTRATION FIVE

Llwyn-on Reservoir

Portraying water can be a challenge in any medium. Like so many aspects of landscape painting the end result benefits enormously from simplification. In this scene an intermittent breeze was blowing, causing a constant change of ripples and reflections across the surface of the water. The furthest part of the reservoir was partly covered with ice.

▶ In my original sketch, much foreground detail had been included – reeds and stones on a spit of land that jutted out into the reservoir. Should I include these? I decided to leave them out, as well as some faint detail on the left-hand bank of conifers. The far right-hand side, however, needed something to balance the composition, so a studio sketch helped me to plot a bank of conifers with attendant reflection.

First Stage

For this painting I chose Waterford 300 gsm (140 lb) Not paper. I began by washing weak Naples Yellow across the sky, leaving a white area in the centre. Whilst this remained wet, I brushed a mixture of French Ultramarine and Cadmium Red over the lower part of the sky and brought it down over the mountains.

At the bottom of the wash I introduced a band of Raw Sienna, adding some Cadmium Yellow Pale in the area where the two large conifers would appear. The aim of this was

to attract the eye towards the focal point.

As the sky dried a little, but was still damp, a stronger fusion of French Ultramarine and Cadmium Red was brought over the top left-hand corner of the sky, then dabbed in across the paper to create a host of small clouds. Note that the brush was only damp – the paint was quite strong with hardly any water on it at this point.

This technique works best when the first wash is just losing its wet sheen. You may find that you run out of time and the wash has dried in places before you can render

Colours

Naples
Yellow

French
Ultramarine

Cadmium
Red

Raw Sienna

Cadmium
Yellow Pale

Light Red

Burnt
Umber

▲ First stage

▶ Second stage

further clouds. Simply let it dry completely and then re-wet the appropriate area with a large soft brush. Again, allow it to partially dry and then finish rendering the clouds.

In order to achieve a sense of unity, the central mountainside was painted with Cadmium Red and French Ultramarine, adding a touch of Raw Sienna and then extending it across to the right. The left-hand mass of conifers was laid with a slightly stronger version of the same mixture, since I wanted this area to come forward more. The whole paper was then allowed to dry before proceeding further.

Second Stage

I used the same mixture on the right-hand tree-clad hill, but I added more water lower down to suggest a soft atmosphere. The left-hand bracken-covered bank needed to

▲ Third stage

come forward to suggest depth, so this was painted with Light Red. However, close to where the trees would appear I splashed in some green and touches of Burnt Umber to define the rocks and to emphasize this section as the centre of interest.

Third Stage

With a combination of French Ultramarine and Burnt Umber the bank of conifers below the right-hand hill were painted in with a No. 4 sable. Note how they stand out slightly more prominently because the lower part of that hill was lightened with water in the second stage – watercolour painting, like chess, benefits from thinking at least one or two moves ahead.

I then strengthened some of the tones on the left-hand bank. To complete this stage I took a large squirrel-hair mop brush and laid a weak mixture of French Ultramarine and Burnt Umber across the reservoir. I then dropped some Naples Yellow into the centre to reflect the colour of the sky.

Finished Stage

I painted in the two pine trees forming the focal point using a strong blend of French Ultramarine and Burnt Umber. Finally, the water was rendered with a weaker mixture of the same colours, leaving the light horizontal slivers. Whilst it was still wet, I put in the dark reflections of the trees to add the finishing touches to the painting.

▲ **Llwyn-on Reservoir, Brecon Beacons**
22 x 33 cm (8¾ x 13 in)

Sunlight and Shadow

Without light there is no form, and unless you carefully consider how light and shadows affect the landscape your work will lack interest. So often you can see a scene which would benefit from sunshine, yet the scene or photograph that you are working from is dull and lifeless. How do you introduce sunlight in these conditions?

Rendering sunlight

Strong sunlight bleaches out detail, produces cast shadows and causes light to be reflected off bright reflective objects. In the early morning and late evening the light casts a warmer glow over the landscape, so at these times you can inject that sense of atmosphere. Strong contrasts and cast shadows will certainly help to give your composition a feeling of sunlight.

Make sure your shadows are consistent throughout the work and that they do not contradict each other. Look for colours within the shadow areas – although they may at first glance appear to be a dismal medium grey, you can often pick out interesting colours that will make the shadows more vibrant and attractive. It is often worth extending a cast shadow just a little bit further than in the original scene to emphasize it further.

If you are attempting to create sunlight which is not actually present, it helps if you draw a tonal sketch to show the shadow and sunlit areas. Colours in sunshine will need to be brightened up and flecks of white paper also help to emphasize the effect.

Detail will be lost in areas that are bathed in sunlight, so keep detail to a minimum here by simply suggesting it. This is readily apparent in photographs, for example, where part of the image is overexposed, so

beware of copying photographs without careful consideration. At times, two walls which are at right angles to each other will be illuminated by sunshine, but one side will usually be slightly darker because the texture is caught at a more acute angle than the other. This applies particularly to heavily textured walls.

Controlling light

By being selective about where you want sunlight to fall, you can accentuate features within the painting. For instance, if you wish to heighten the drama of a crag, or perhaps highlight a specific tree, you can place the feature within a light patch and create an area of shadow around it to spotlight the focal point. Of course, it helps if the sky and atmosphere correspond with the lighting effects – a clear blue sky would

▲ **Pembridge, Herefordshire**
16 x 21 cm (6¼ x 8¼ in)
Cast shadows are the most potent way of suggesting sunlight, but make sure they are all facing the same direction! Note the white reflected light to the left of the chimney on the right-hand building.

◀ Rocks catch the light easily because they have reflective surfaces. Here, a dark background shows up the lightness of the top of the rock. Build up rocks in stages and begin with the actual rock colours, which often change and blend into one another. When the first wash is dry, paint any textures and shadows. Finally, detail in the strongest tones of the fissures and darkest shadows.

be out of place, for example, because a 'spotlight' would need to come through the clouds.

Dark washes laid horizontally across the foreground suggest a sunlit middle and far distance – this could be the result of cloud shadow or the shadows cast by a tree or a building just out of the picture area.

Repaint a scene that ended up rather dull and try to inject a sense of strong sunlight into the new version. Alternatively, work from a dull sketch or photograph that would benefit from brightening up.

◀ **Loch Coire nan Arr and Sgurr a' Ghaorachain**
19 x 27 cm (7½ x 10½ in)
On a sombre day in the Applecross Mountains a sudden break in the cloud cover brought a cascade of sunlight onto the crags above the loch. By emphasizing the darkness all around, the crags really stand out as the focal point. To help achieve the sparkle on the water and the ground texture I used Waterford Rough 640 gsm (300 lb).

Cottage at Kinnersley

This lovely old black and white cottage, unfortunately, looked down onto another garden encompassed within ranch-style fencing that seemed out of keeping with this subject. This was further complicated by the need to create a lead-in to the cottage. I also needed to brighten up what was a particularly dull day and bring some sunshine into the painting.

▶ First stage

Colours

Cadmium Yellow Pale

Cobalt Blue

Cadmium Red

Raw Sienna

Burnt Umber

French Ultramarine

Light Red

Cadmium Yellow Deep

First Stage

I drew the subject in pencil outline on Waterford Not 410 gsm (200 lb). Then I applied masking fluid to most of the white areas that would be catching the sunlight, which I intended to come from the right. The masking fluid was allowed a few minutes to dry thoroughly before beginning on the painting.

The sky was completely wetted with clean water. A weak wash of Cadmium Yellow Pale was then brushed onto the lower sky, with a stronger version across the right-hand field. Without pausing, a wash of Cobalt Blue mixed with Cadmium Red was painted onto the top part of the sky and a slightly stronger mix of the same colours across the bottom of the sky. I added a fluid wash of Raw Sienna to cover the foreground – I left some parts untouched to give a sense of liveliness to the painting.

When all the washes were dry the distant trees and hedgerow were rendered with a medium-strength blend of Cobalt Blue and Burnt Umber. I often use Cobalt Blue for weaker distant features and French

100

◄ Second stage

Ultramarine where stronger mixes are required. In this case, I resorted to French Ultramarine with Light Red for the left-hand bushes, allowing the red colour to dominate and to imply dead leaves.

Second Stage

The trees were defined with a French Ultramarine and Light Red combination. After the masking fluid was removed I added the shadows with a mixture of French Ultramarine and Cadmium Red. Light Red was applied to define the chimneys. The strong detail on the windows was painted in with French Ultramarine and Burnt Umber.

Once the chimneys were dry, a mixture of Cadmium Yellow Deep and French Ultramarine was laid across the roof, with some stronger Light Red and Cadmium Yellow Deep dropped in in several places to add some variation.

Third Stage

Further detail was added to the roof and house before the hedgerow colours of Cadmium Yellow Pale and French Ultramarine were painted in, with Light Red dropped in here and there to suggest

▲ Third stage

variety. Too much detail in a hedgerow can have a tendency to make it look over-laboured, so introducing a change in colour is an excellent substitute for detail.

The gates were then defined, mainly using the colours French Ultramarine and Burnt Umber. Below the hedgerow, I painted a wash of Raw Sienna and French Ultramarine with a little Cadmium Yellow Pale in places.

◀ **Cottage at Kinnersley, Herefordshire**
23 x 33 cm (9 x 13 in)

Finished Stage

Finally, I applied a few more details to sharpen up some features and laid a dark wash of Burnt Umber and French Ultramarine over the foreground in order to accentuate the light around the cottage. When this was dry I picked out a few stones and some detail in the immediate foreground.

▼ Detail of finished painting

People, Birds and Animals

Many scenes, such as towns, villages and harbours, call out for figures, otherwise a painting can take on a 'ghost town' look. In other types of scenery figures and animals can be used as a focal point, or in support of the focal point, and there are many scenes where some form of life will enhance the work. Therefore, at some stage, you will find it worthwhile including figures or animals in your paintings. Because they do not need to be very big, rendering them is not as difficult as it might sound.

Figures

Figures are powerful tools in a painting because they draw the eye immediately to themselves. Consider figures at the design stage and pencil them in carefully. Make sure that they are in proportion with their surroundings; for example, can they get through that door?

Try to have them doing something, rather than just standing, and make sure they are in character with their environment. Ease off on the detail immediately around figures otherwise they become lost in their surroundings, especially in a complicated section of a composition.

In mountain scenes it is often difficult to know whether to include walkers and climbers, since they can be intrusive to some viewers. On the other hand, they are able to provide a marvellous sense of scale – a lone walker really can make a painting feel desolate if that is what you are aiming for.

If you are unsure about including a figure, paint one in and see how it looks. If it seems out of place, quickly wash it out with a wet brush, dabbing the paper dry with a tissue. Unless you are using staining

Cwm-y-glo main street

colours, such as Crimson Alizarin or Viridian, it should wash off. If you experience any problems, try turning the figure into a rock, tree or bush, for example.

Birds

Chickens, cockerels and pheasants can breathe a sense of colour and life into a painting and they can even form the focal point. Birds in flight also tend to help lend a sense of life. Seagulls are excellent for giving

▶ Chickens can bring a wonderful sense of life to a farm scene, so it is worth sketching a few in pencil and colour.

▲ Avoid describing any detail immediately around figures – give them plenty of space, as shown in this sketch – otherwise they simply become lost in the scene.

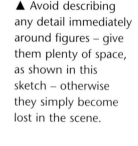

▶ **Cattle in the Shade**
14 x 24 cm (5½ x 9½ in)
Animals make a superb centre of interest, even when they are quite small within the composition. In this painting they relieve the overwhelming greenery of summer foliage. The paper used was Bockingford Not 410 gsm (200 lb).

a sense of height and drama to a cliff, and they can be rendered dark against a light sky or light against a darker cliff. In the latter case I normally use white gouache for the gulls. Masses of gulls following a boat or tractor ploughing a field can impart a real feeling of movement and dynamism.

Animals

By including a few animals, in fields, for example, you can make a painting come alive. Cattle are especially suitable because they are more angular and easier to draw than horses. Generally, they stand out well against backgrounds, particularly the black and white Friesians.

Sheep, though fairly easy to draw, are sometimes difficult to see in a painting with a light field. As the painter's tonal range is more restricted than that of nature, you have to make the field a little darker in tone than it is in reality. In this way the light-coloured sheep will be more visible. It is also best not to spread the animals all over a field, but to group them together.

◀ **Preseli Farm, Pembrokeshire**
19 x 32 cm (7½ x 12½ in)
Naples Yellow is an excellent colour for painting sheep. Here I have dropped a few spots of Raw Sienna into Naples Yellow whilst the sheep were still wet.

Wiltshire Farm

I came across this lovely old farm whilst out on a walk. The main farmyard stood behind me as I sketched, knee-deep in mud. It was teeming with chickens and cattle and seemed the perfect subject for my sketchbook and pencil. A mass of wild vegetation separated me from the farmhouse, but most of the detail could still be seen.

Colours

 Coeruleum Blue

 Cadmium Red

 Naples Yellow

 French Ultramarine

 Light Red

 Raw Sienna

 Cadmium Yellow Pale

First Stage

I washed Coeruleum Blue across the sky, leaving some white cloud areas. Whilst this was still wet I laid on a mixture of Coeruleum Blue and Cadmium Red lower down, with some splashes of Naples Yellow in places.

Second Stage

For the stronger left-hand cloud I chose a mixture of French Ultramarine and Cadmium Red, softening the edge in places

▲ First stage

with a damp brush. Once this was dry the background trees were painted in with French Ultramarine and Light Red, using a No. 6 round brush on its side to create a more random effect, dry-brush style. Lower down I increased the water content slightly to help suggest a greater mass of trees. Whilst this remained wet I rapidly indicated some of the main trunks to produce a soft effect.

◀ Second stage

The walls and chimneys were painted in with Light Red. A mixture of Raw Sienna and French Ultramarine was used to render both the parked vehicle and the bush by the outbuilding. These did not actually exist in the original scene, but they were added to create additional interest.

Third Stage

Using a No. 6 round brush I painted the shadow sides of the walls with Light Red and French Ultramarine. When these were dry, I suggested the windows with a darker mixture of the same colours. For the bushes I used mainly Raw Sienna, with dabs of Light Red in places. Dropping warm colours into vegetation is an effective device for introducing some variation and interest. I then produced a green by mixing French Ultramarine, Raw Sienna and some Cadmium Yellow Pale, and laid it across the grassy areas.

▶ Third stage

▲ Detail of finished painting

Finished Stage

The bushes were completed by introducing some shadow. I then added the chickens, figures and cow parsley using a No. 4 round brush, although a No. 1 rigger was used for the finest work. The detail was strengthened in several places before laying a foreground wash of French Ultramarine and Light Red to give the painting more depth. I then spattered the foreground by dragging a knife blade across a toothbrush loaded with a darker version of the same mixture. Finally, I flicked in a few larger dabs to suggest the rough ground.

◀ **Wiltshire Farm**
23 x 30 cm (9 x 12 in)

Sketching on Location

Once you have gained some experience in working from the paintings that are featured in this part of the book, you will inevitably wish to seek out subjects of your own. Whilst many artists feel that it is easier to paint from photographs, you will learn more quickly if you take a sketchbook outdoors and learn to observe nature.

Try not to be too ambitious to start with: sallying forth with an easel, a large board and a box of paints announces you as an artist to the world, and you will rapidly be surrounded by many people offering the most amazing advice.

First steps

Begin with an A5 cartridge sketchbook and a few well-sharpened 3B or 4B pencils. If you feel timid venturing outdoors, you can hide your sketchpad within a magazine and

wear a large wide-brimmed hat. This tends to isolate you from any onlookers. I have found that a few violent sneezes can discourage even the most determined critics!

Look for a subject that has a definite focal point, such as a cottage, a waterfall or an interesting tree. Walk around for a few moments to find the best view of the subject, then start drawing the feature that excited you most when you first saw the scene and work outwards.

Draw lightly to begin with to make sure that you include the whole subject, then restate the detail more strongly. Try to avoid constant rubbing out – it is usually easier to apply the pencil strokes strongly once you are confident of the composition and working over any mistakes, rather than pummelling the paper into submission.

When working in monochrome, do make notes about the main colours. Do not be

▼ **Fron Farm, Pant-y-dwr, Mid Wales** 15 x 28 cm (6 x 11 in) It is useful to filter out unnecessary clutter when sketching. I eased off the detail at the left-hand end of the buildings so that the fence and cow would stand out.

▶ After making a number of sketches of this old barn in County Galway, Ireland, I decided to capture the amazing detail that surrounded what was left of this old door. At one point, a rusty old iron kettle had also been pressed into use to hold down the roof. Do go in close to your subject to sketch any interesting detail.

Under the pole and above the door is fixed a sheet of flattened, rusty corrugated iron

← Two poles holding
← down the corrugated
iron roof, with
stones balanced on
top for more weight

The hanging larger
stones also add
weight to the
poles, the wire
rusting in places

Old Farmhouse.
Tnagh Valley, Connemara

afraid to scribble these notes on the sketch because it should be regarded as a working document rather than a finished work of art in itself.

Consider what you will need to make a painting out of your sketch and perhaps include more detail than you feel you might need. This way, if you do work on a much larger scale when painting the final version, you will be better armed. This is particularly important if you are away at some distant holiday location. Taking some back-up photographs is also helpful.

Constant comparison

By comparing the various features against each other you will gain a much better understanding of a scene. Does that roof appear darker than the background hill? Where does the line of the eaves of the adjacent barn meet the main house? Which side of the building is catching the most light? If a figure is to be included, how high should it appear?

Steer away from relying on lines to define each object by using tones to make the features stand out against each other, although in places it helps to make some of

them merge into one another. In particular, compare the tones on the distant hills or trees with those at the focal point and the actual foreground.

Sketching in colour

Once you have had some experience of sketching with pencil, try charcoal, pens, watersoluble pencils and, once you feel like tackling it, watercolour. A lot can be achieved with a compact box of paints that

▼ **Allt Meallan Gobhar, Applecross**
14 x 20 cm (5½ x 8 in)
Amidst lashing rain, I used a blue-grey watercolour pencil for the background area, much of which was washed off. The black watercolour pencil used on the closer features brought a sense of depth into the sketch.

can be kept in a large handbag or waist bag. A good quality cartridge pad, such as the Lyndhurst, can take washes or pencil, but you may well want to graduate to a spiral-bound watercolour pad. The temptation can then be to produce an almost finished watercolour rather than a sketch.

However, the important thing is to start painting outdoors because it helps your general watercolour techniques a great deal. Outside, of course, you can always blame the elements, the onlookers or even the wild dogs for any mistakes!

There is no need to slavishly record every colour you see. There will no doubt be countless greens to reproduce if you are working in the summertime, so reduce them to a manageable three, or four at most. When the sun appears, make full use of it to create shadows and a sense of sunlight – it might not last long. On dull days, you can emphasize the three-dimensional quality of buildings by making one wall darker than the other, otherwise your painting will appear flat. Accentuate any highlights by making full use of the white of the paper.

Try to include some figures and animals because they can breathe life into a painting

▶ **Farm above Bethesda, Snowdonia**
22 x 33 cm (8¾ x 13 in)
Try to bring out the character of the subject by focusing on local idiosyncrasies. This scene is on the edge of the great Penrhyn quarry in Wales that has large waste heaps of slate. The fencing in front of the cottage is made from large slivers of slate, which stood out particularly well against a dark backdrop. I enjoy doing colour sketches like this on cartridge paper.

▶ **Powder Mills Farm, Dartmoor**
20 x 33 cm (8 x 13 in)
In this simple watercolour sketch, painted on cartridge paper, runbacks have formed in the sky, but in a way they seem to enhance it. I used a black watercolour pencil to suggest the detail, so I was able to finish the sketch in a few minutes without interruption.

and act as the focal point if there is no strong centre of interest. They are often best sketched in at the side of the sheet you are working on, or on another page, and then added separately into your watercolour. In a landscape, you do not need to make them large and, therefore, they do not have to be highly detailed.

If you still feel inhibited when working outdoors, try sketching from a car or a café, or with your back to a wall, to make it difficult for anyone to view your work. Sketching can be the most enjoyable of activities all year round as long as you are properly equipped, so do make a go of it.

Working from Photographs

There are many artists who work not only from other people's photographs, but from postcards, calendars, magazines and the television screen. Others would not think of using even their own photographs. For the housebound and infirm, working from a variety of sources may be the only possible course of action and, indeed, many people are unable to regularly get out to view the landscapes they would dearly love to paint.

Ideally, working directly from the landscape is best – sketching is the most enjoyable of all my activities – but you should not ignore the camera as a powerful tool in producing rapid images. Sometimes there is just not enough time to render a mass of detail with a pencil, so photographs can help enormously to fill in the missing pieces or to check the steepness of a particular hill.

Taking landscape snapshots

Many people are disappointed with their photographs and sometimes cannot even see the focal point that looked so interesting in the original scene. With compact cameras, in particular, the image is flattened and pushed back with the wide-angle lens. By using a zoom lens, you can close in on

◄ Happily, this traditional tigh geal (white house) is lived in though, aesthetically, the car and modern gate did little to enhance the appeal. They would have to be omitted from the final painting.

◄ Even though I had an original pencil sketch available, for the purposes of this exercise I wanted to produce a studio tonal sketch from the photograph. Sky detail was totally lacking in the photograph. I also wanted to enhance the water and reduce the effect of the long boring whaleback ridge in the distance. The distant buildings were distracting, so they were left out.

your focal point in one shot and zoom out to get the setting in the next. Close-up shots are vital for capturing detail.

As with sketching, moving around and waiting for the right light will greatly improve your photographs. Look at the scene for a few moments and take your time before taking the shot to analyse potential areas of confusion and to consider the best angle. Photographs taken from slightly different angles can help enormously to ascertain what bit of detail – a chimney perhaps – belongs to what feature.

Look also for the interesting minor features, such as gateposts, tractors and farm animals. Even if these items are photographed separately, they can still be added to a composition. Sky detail usually suffers in photographs – if the sky is interesting, take a separate shot of it, exposing for the sky alone.

Painting from photographs

Try not to copy photographs slavishly because it can make the final painting appear rather wooden. It is a good idea to carry out a sketch from the photograph, then putting the photograph aside and simply painting from the sketch. The resulting image will probably be more lively.

Photographs generally need to be simplified by reducing the amount of detail. Don't feel the urge to copy every colour because this can destroy the sense of unity in a painting. Perhaps most of all, you need to be aware that the tones may well need to be modified if the light was poor when the photograph was taken. Improving this aspect does need experience. By all means use photographs when you have to, but do try to work directly from nature whenever the opportunity arises.

▼**Tigh Geal, North Uist**
22 x 34 cm (8½ x 13½ in)
Here the ridge has been effectively reduced by low cloud, but a patch of blue sky in the centre cheers up the scene. I added sparkle to the water by dragging French Ultramarine horizontally across the paper. The wall to the left of the cottage has been raised slightly and the outbuilding strengthened to bring it forward of the cottage. I also brought the track down a little to involve the foreground.

Skies in Watercolour
By Ron Ranson

Without doubt, painting skies is one of my greatest joys. Like everything else worth doing, creating authentic skies will require practice while you are learning the new skills you need, but you'll soon find that all the effort you have put in will be well rewarded. You'll notice that your painting will take on vitality, excitement and atmosphere, giving endless satisfaction, not only to you, but to your viewers also.

However, it does seem to me that skies are the most neglected area of landscape painting. So much time is spent learning how to paint trees, rivers and buildings that the sky is often just filled in as an afterthought. This is strange when you consider that the sky is not only an integral part of the landscape, but actually affects the whole scene below it. Many teachers of watercolour, both in their workshops and in the instructional books

they write, leave too little time or space to explore this important aspect of creating convincing and memorable paintings.

Changing the mood

If you look at the two illustrations on these pages and then imagine the weather conditions reversed, both pictures would change dramatically. None of the main features would be removed and yet the whole scene would present an altered aspect.

For an element that is always with us, most of us know appallingly little about skies. Cloud types are generally unknown, and without at least basic knowledge, convincing skies in your paintings are unattainable. The good news is that the techniques you need for painting skies are easily learned, and watercolour is the ideal medium to use.

▼ **More Snow on the Way**
31 x 41 cm (12 x 16 in)
This is a scene of contrasts. The softly painted, wet-into-wet sky, threatening snow, contrasts with the crisp trees in the middle distance. The snow, represented by the white of the paper, is highlighted against the dark foreground rocks.

Achieving atmosphere

I'm hoping first of all to show you the basic cloud types and then, by a mixture of example and instruction, to help you achieve atmospheric skies that will enhance the whole of your landscape painting. To be honest, 90 per cent of the secret is the water content of your brush, and this is a practical exercise that can easily be learned. Once you have mastered the technique, there is nothing like the pleasure of watching a watercolour sky materializing in front of your eyes. The other 10 per cent is to avoid at all costs overworking, which produces muddy, tired skies. My constant cry in my workshops is: 'Leave it alone! Let the watercolour work by itself.'

Having helped hundreds of students in the past through my workshops, I have no doubt that you, too, will succeed in painting skies. What you do need is plenty of practice. Use the backs of some of your less successful paintings. Be courageous – this isn't a time for timidity.

On the next two pages, I'm going to give you basic information on cloud types, and throughout the other chapters in this section of the book, I will try to cover all the other aspects of painting watercolour skies. Read on and then have a go.

▲ **Cumulus over the Fields**
29 x 40 cm (11½ x 15½ in)
White, fluffy cumulus clouds are exciting as they move majestically over the landscape. Notice how the sky colour is repeated in the foreground.

The more emotionally involved you are with your painting, the more successful you will be.

117

Understanding Skies

You don't have to be a meteorologist to paint convincing skies, but you will require a basic knowledge of the most usual cloud types. The skies above us are constantly changing, presenting artists with quite a challenge. However, it is this constant change that has provided inspiration for landscape and seascape painters over the centuries.

Cloud formations

Although there are about ten major cloud formations, it isn't necessary for you to become closely involved with all of them – though having said that, there is always the danger that you will get hooked and want to learn more and more! The basic cloud formations that, as a painter, you really do need to know about are only four. Their names, derived from the Latin, also act as descriptions and are as follows:

> Cumulus: Heap
> Cirrus: Fringe or thread
> Stratus: Layer
> Nimbus: Rain

Once you have identified these four (and you'll get help with recognition from the photographs shown here) and become familiar with them, you'll find skies increasingly fascinating. Of course, you're seldom going to be able to look up and find one perfectly illustrated cloud form in an otherwise clear sky. Most of the time, you will see the various cloud types overlapping at their different levels. Even so, you'll be able to pick out the basic four quite easily.

▲ Cumulus

indicators of fair weather with no immediate change. Perhaps the most important thing to remember about them is that they have rounded tops and flatter bottoms. When painting these clouds, be aware that perspective is well defined, with the clouds rapidly getting smaller as they reach the horizon. Their shape is moulded by the light of the sun, the tops often being brilliant white, while the base is in subtle shadow – very exciting to paint.

Cumulus

If you look up and see these fluffy 'cotton wool' clouds in a blue sky, you've no excuse not to go out and paint them, as they are

Cirrus

These feathery clouds, often called 'mares' tails', appear high in a blue sky. At about 9,000 metres (30,000 feet), cirrus is the

▲ Cirrus

▲ Stratus

▲ Nimbus

highest cloud form, perhaps looking at its best in the evening in the dying rays of the sun. A different form of cirrus is sometimes seen in the light, delicate ripples known as a 'mackerel sky'. In painting cirrus clouds, a subtle and delicate touch is required – they can be used to great advantage when contrasted with stronger, more dramatic cumulus clouds beneath them. This cloud type is very useful in breaking up the monotony of a plain blue sky without being dominant and distracting from the rest of the painting.

Stratus

The most obvious characteristic of stratus is its horizontal, layered appearance, with the clouds continuing into the distance in diminishing rows. The light source is often visible and can produce dramatic effects, particularly when shafts of light shine through gaps in the cloud. If the sun is visible through the cloud, its outline can be clearly seen. In a painting, the light source can be used to avoid monotony of colour.

Nimbus

These clouds actually come in two forms. One is the cumulo-nimbus cloud, which is heavy and dense, and either extends horizontally or forms huge towers. The other, known as nimbo-stratus, forms a grey cloud layer. As both these clouds usually indicate that it is raining or snowing, they're probably best viewed from inside.

Nimbus are the darkest and heaviest cloud forms, but even so, you must take care not to make them too dark in your paintings. This is because the landscape beneath always appears darker than the clouds themselves, and so you would end up with a painting devoid of form and colour.

Watercolour Techniques

Painting skies is all about applying washes, and most of the problems you will encounter will be involved with getting the water content right. Not only the water content of your brush at the time of application, but the amount of dampness still left on the paper when you put on the next wash – in other words, timing. This is not something that will take months to achieve, but you won't learn just by reading about it. It is something that needs practical application.

When teaching, I usually find that my students master the water content/timing problem in about an hour-and-a-half. Like ice skating and riding a bike, it may look impossible, but a little application and a few falls work wonders! All that is needed in addition is confidence, and this again you will only acquire through practice.

Working wet-into-wet

You will find the hake brush ideal for skies, as it covers the paper so quickly and delicately. Practise with the brush, using it as lightly as

possible and working with your whole arm rather than just from the wrist. I have provided a few examples of sky mixtures on these pages for you to copy, so that you can get the feel of applying the washes. Don't expect to be able to reproduce them exactly; this is impossible. Instead, use them to help you to understand the wet-into-wet technique.

When using wet-into-wet, it's necessary to work on a slope, so that the washes flow into one another. Try various angles for different

▲ To create a straight-forward graduated sky, put on an overall wash of watery Raw Sienna, followed immediately by a wash of French Ultramarine across the top. Gradually take the pressure off the brush as you work downwards with the Ultramarine.

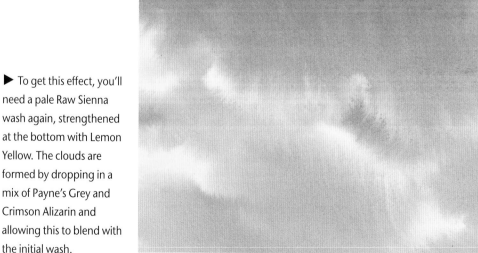

▶ To get this effect, you'll need a pale Raw Sienna wash again, strengthened at the bottom with Lemon Yellow. The clouds are formed by dropping in a mix of Payne's Grey and Crimson Alizarin and allowing this to blend with the initial wash.

◀ For this sky, graduate some blue over the usual pale Raw Sienna wash at the top and put in a mix of Crimson Alizarin and Lemon Yellow at the bottom. Immediately drop in a strong mixture of Payne's Grey and Crimson Alizarin for the dark clouds.

▲ After your pale Raw Sienna wash, paint around the cloud shapes with Prussian Blue, leaving the first wash to show through. Now paint in the dark clouds with Payne's Grey and Crimson Alizarin.

▲ A slightly more ambitious sky here, using the usual Raw Sienna followed by French Ultramarine in the top left-hand corner, and blending Lemon Yellow and Crimson Alizarin at the bottom. Put in the darker clouds with Payne's Grey and Crimson Alizarin.

effects – the exercises shown here were carried out on a 45 degree slope, allowing gravity to help! Put a first wash on your paper with very weak paint. Then dry your brush, mix some rich, strong paint and apply it immediately on top of the first, still damp, wash. Then stand back and just watch what happens!

One of the most important things to remember is to compensate for the dampness already on the paper from your first wash. To do this, you must make your second application thicker and richer than you would consider necessary. Frighten yourself when you put the paint on. It probably won't look right at first, but after about a minute, as it softens and diffuses, you will see authentic cloud shapes appearing. All very exciting and rewarding!

Don't attempt to complete a painting here – simply regard these exercises as an experiment in judging water content. You will learn more through trial and error than any other way.

a

◀ Try copying the four little vignettes on this page, using only the hake brush. Experiment, bearing in mind the water content of the brush.

a Drop in the reflection of the tree while the water area is still damp.

b Paint the mauve area right across in a weak wash. Then immediately paint in the nearer trees with thicker paint on top.

c These tree reflections are again painted wet-into-wet.

d The trees here are put in with a fairly dry brush, while the foreground shadows on the snow are stroked in very quickly and lightly.

Brush techniques

Now that you have seen how to use the hake brush to create washes for the sky, let's look at other ways in which this brush can be used effectively in the rest of the landscape. Apart from the hake, the other brushes that I normally use – the 25 mm (1 in) flat brush and the rigger – are each ideal for certain landscape features.

Using a hake

Imagine first that you want to show hills on the horizon. If you're aiming to portray a wet or misty day, you'll need to put in the hills before the sky has quite dried to convey a soft appearance. If on the other hand, you're painting a blue sky with sparkling cumulus clouds, then you must wait until the sky is completely dry, so that the hills will appear clear and sharp to enhance the atmosphere of a sunny day. Impatience will be your greatest enemy here.
Putting in

c

your horizon too quickly will ruin an otherwise perfectly good sky.

As you move forward in the scene, you may want to put in fields, trees and hedges. Distant fields can be indicated by swift horizontal strokes of the brush, while distant trees can be put in with downward strokes of a corner of the brush. Rough scrub land in the foreground can be produced by fast strokes of the hake combined with flicks of a fingernail. Try using your knuckles too, in a wet wash, to produce foreground texture.

d

b

In this illustration of a harbour view, you can see how the 25 mm (1 in) flat brush can produce crisp lines as well as hard-edged objects.

Using a 25 mm (1 in) flat brush

You'll find the 25 mm (1 in) flat brush invaluable in your landscapes – as with the hake, use it with delicacy. The almost knife-like edge will allow you to put in features such as railings, gates, doorways, windows, masts and distant boats. In other words, you can use this brush wherever a sharp edge is required. The 25 mm (1 in) flat comes into its own, too, for indicating distant buildings and sheds.

Take a look at the illustration above, then have a go at using the brush yourself. Soon you'll be producing authentic, yet economical detail in your scene.

Using a rigger

This is another brush that will become indispensable. The amount of pressure is paramount here. The long hair means that, by varying the pressure, you will be able to produce marks ranging from a hair's width to about 6 mm (¼ in). Try holding the brush right at the end of the handle to give you more flexibility of stroke. For a tapering line, move just your fingers rather than the whole hand.

Use the brush for features as diverse as figures, grasses, winter trees and birds. Tree branches in all seasons are best painted with the rigger; try to achieve the uniformly tapering effect so important for authenticity.

▲ To paint this winter tree you will need plenty of practice at holding the rigger at the very end of the handle. Getting enough taper is the aim here.

▲ When painting figures with a rigger, keep them very simple with no features, hands or feet. The most important thing is to make the heads small (an adult figure is about seven heads high).

▲ Using a rigger for birds is simplicity itself! But don't overdo it, and vary the sizes to give the impression of distance.

◀ Quick flicks of the rigger give the effect of blades of grass.

Creating highlights

The following techniques will show you how to introduce highlights and sparkle to your paintings. This is an area where a preliminary tonal sketch (see page 140) will help you to decide where these highlights can be used to the greatest advantage.

Dry brush technique

This technique reproduces effects such as sparkle on water or texture on a road, and works best on Not or rough paper rather than smooth paper. The secret is to put your brush stroke in quickly and lightly on the dry surface of the paper. The paint will be left just on the raised parts of the surface, while the indents remain untouched.

Practise this method of working over and over again on scrap paper until you are pleased with the result. The same technique can be used over a previous wash (once the wash has dried) to create textural effects, perhaps in a foreground. To avoid giving your foregrounds an overly bitty appearance, you can simplify them by standing up and using your whole arm to sweep the brush lightly across the paper.

▲ **Cirrus over an Oregon Lake**
31 x 41 cm (12 x 16 in)
Here, the sparkle was created by painting a wash of Prussian Blue very quickly and lightly over the lake area. The brush just skimmed over the top surface of the paper, leaving the indented areas untouched.

Leaving white paper

The whiteness of the paper is a very important part of painting in watercolour, and there are many occasions when leaving the paper untouched is the best way to produce certain effects. You may wish to portray snow on a mountain or a white house backed by dark trees, for example. You will need to plan these areas beforehand and paint carefully around the desired shapes.

Masking fluid

Perhaps an easier method of leaving your white shape is to paint it first with masking fluid, giving the fluid time to dry before starting your painting. Once the watercolour itself has completely dried, the masking fluid can easily be rubbed off with your finger, leaving the required shape untouched.

◀ The areas of shadow on the snow were very lightly painted in a mix of Payne's Grey and Crimson Alizarin to match the sky, unifying the two elements. The white paper left showing effectively suggests the brighter patches of snow on the fields.

▶ The area of the castle was painted with masking fluid, using an old brush. Once the masking fluid had dried, the sky was washed in with abandon. When the sky was quite dry, the masking fluid was rubbed off and the castle was completed.

Wiping out

A light, soft streak, perhaps on the surface of water, can be achieved by a sideways, horizontal stroke of a clean, dry hake while the wash is still damp. This is most effective against the darkest part of the water.

For a sharp-edged shape, such as the sail of a yacht, lay two pieces of paper together at an angle on top of the painting and gently rub the surface between them with a damp hog's hair oil-painting brush. I find that a bit of spit on a tissue works well, too – especially on Bockingford paper. Both these methods require patience and delicacy. You'll see examples of yacht sails created by this technique on pages 145 and 151.

◀ Immediately after painting in the reflected mountain, the hake brush was dried on a rag to make it 'thirsty'. Making a horizontal sweep with the edge of the brush gave the impression of a wind-driven patch of water.

Exploring Colour

As you begin to explore and experiment with colour, it is best to use just a few paints and get to know them really well. Learn how they mix with each other and also how they mix with water – in other words, learn how to make the best possible use of them. Given time and practice, with just a few colours you will soon be producing all the shades you need for your paintings.

An important thing to remember when mixing colours is to keep your paints clean. Often you'll produce the required colour by mixing only two of your originals. Try to work in this way, particularly in the early days, as you will avoid muddiness and ensure freshness. If you have white paint in your selection, never mix it with another colour, as it will only produce a milky opaqueness that will destroy the transparency of watercolour.

Don't be afraid to use watercolour boldly and with courage. Nothing looks worse than a washed-out, weak painting.

| Lemon Yellow | Raw Sienna | French Ultramarine | Light Red |
| Payne's Grey | Burnt Umber | Crimson Alizarin | Prussian Blue |

◀ This little painting, although subtle in colour, actually contains mixes of all the eight colours shown above.

Harmonious colours

The illustration on the right shows harmonious colours. These are colours that are closely related, such as orange and red, or green and yellow. Used judiciously, they will always give a sense of peace and pleasure.

Complementary colours

Complementary colours are contrasting colours that are directly opposite each other on the spectrum – for example, red and green, or blue and orange. They can be invaluable in enlivening a painting. A predominantly green landscape, for instance, will come to life with the addition of a touch of light red.

▲ The use of harmonious colours evokes a tranquil atmosphere in this woodland scene.

◀ Complementary colours can be used in a painting to draw attention to a particular area, such as the red roof amidst the green foliage.

Warm and cool colours

Warm and cool colours are tremendously useful in a painting. Warm colours will always appear to advance when placed near cool colours. Conversely, cool colours will appear to recede when used near warm colours. You will be able to exploit these qualitites to great effect to convey space and recession in your painting by using warm colours in the foreground of your scene and cool colours for distant objects.

◀ Notice here how the warm rich colours of the foreground rock push back the cool colours of the distant hills.

127

Colours for skies

Let's look now at sky painting in particular. Virtually every sky portrayed in this book is built up from the following colours: Raw Sienna, Payne's Grey, Crimson Alizarin, Lemon Yellow, French Ultramarine, Prussian Blue and Light Red. As I said earlier, you can add to these to suit your taste, but as you need to concentrate on the varied water content and the timing of each part of the sky, you can see the advantage of limiting your colours.

Here are some basic skies with swatches showing the colours used to paint them.

Clear sky
The clear blue sky in the first illustration must be graduated to look effective. Applied over a very weak wash of Raw Sienna, a rich French Ultramarine gradually becomes paler from the top to the bottom of the sky, until the colour fades to a light cream at the horizon.

Cumulus clouds
Once again, a very pale Raw Sienna forms the basic wash across the sky area. French Ultramarine, painted around the cloud shape, forms the blue of the sky, leaving the cream colour to suggest the cloud itself. The shadowed base of the cloud is a mix of Payne's Grey and a little Crimson Alizarin.

Cloudy sky
After the usual very pale Raw Sienna wash, the clouds are painted in quickly with a mix of Payne's Grey and Crimson Alizarin – the same mix as used for the base of the cloud in the cumulus sky.

Sunset
After the initial wash of Raw Sienna, a brush full of French Ultramarine creates a darker tone across the top of the sky. The touches of pink and yellow typical of a sunset are added with Crimson Alizarin and Lemon Yellow, put on in varying strengths and allowed to blend. The clouds are a stronger mixture of Payne's Grey and Crimson Alizarin.

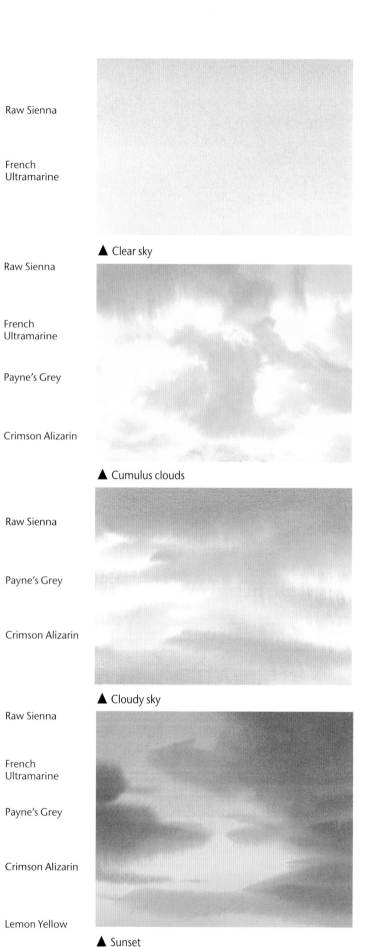

Raw Sienna

French Ultramarine

Raw Sienna

French Ultramarine

Payne's Grey

Crimson Alizarin

Raw Sienna

Payne's Grey

Crimson Alizarin

Raw Sienna

French Ultramarine

Payne's Grey

Crimson Alizarin

Lemon Yellow

▲ Clear sky

▲ Cumulus clouds

▲ Cloudy sky

▲ Sunset

Landscape colours

You can't avoid learning how to mix a good range of greens for the landscapes beneath your skies. The whole range can be obtained by using blue, yellow, grey and Raw Sienna.

On this page, I've demonstrated how to obtain the effect of distance by using cool blue-greens in the background, and building up to rich, warm greens in the foreground. The dark, rich greens are mixed with much less water. Try mixing the range of greens on some scraps of paper first, then move on to copying the illustrations.

▼ This vignette uses the whole spectrum of greens.

Turning to earth shades, there are greens here too, but now you need to move towards warmer foreground colours mixed from the range shown below. Again, practise copying these on to spare paper to get the feeling of the colours. You'll soon find that different colours will vary the atmosphere in your paintings.

▲ To obtain this range of greens, you'll need to start at the back with French Ultramarine and the merest touch of yellow, then gradually add more yellow as you move forwards. Once you have applied the brightest green, begin to add Payne's Grey until you reach the darkest green in the foreground, which contains much less water.

▼ There is still plenty of green in this landscape, but with added touches of Burnt Umber and Light Red.

▶ Useful earth colours can be mixed from (left to right) Raw Sienna, Light Red, Burnt Umber and French Ultramarine.

Simple Skies

The time has come for you to have a go at some complete skies yourself. Some of the different sky types are set out on these four pages for you to copy. Arm yourself with lots of paper, perhaps paper that you've already used on one side. Remember that you'll get the best results if you work with your board at an angle of about 45 degrees.

If your skies don't work first time, don't be discouraged – just enjoy experimenting with the paint and water. It may take several attempts before you achieve the right water content which will make your skies believable. A few initial disasters are all part of the learning process!

Clear sky

1 Using a hake, paint an extremely weak wash of Raw Sienna over the whole sky area. It should appear as a very pale cream colour.

2 Now mix up a rich wash of French Ultramarine and immediately, while the first wash is still wet, put in a band of the blue right across the top of the page.

3 Continue putting the Ultramarine in, using your whole arm to move the brush backwards and forwards, and gradually taking the pressure off the brush as you work down the sky. Now stand back and watch. If you've got it right, gravity will take out any streaks and you will be left with a lovely, clear, graduated sky after a couple of minutes. If you haven't achieved this effect, try again!

◀ 1

▼ 3

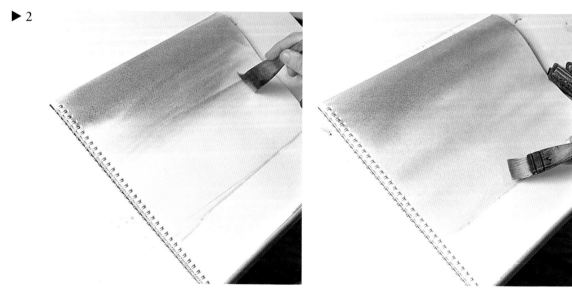

▶ 2

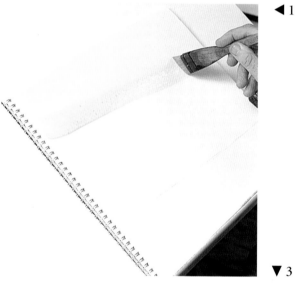

130

Cirrus sky

1 As in the previous example, put on a very pale wash of Raw Sienna. With rich French Ultramarine, immediately use your hake to begin making streaks across the sky in a curve.

2 Continue adding Ultramarine – it is really important to use your whole arm to get a smooth sweep of colour. Note that the blue is creating negative shapes, and the original wash showing through is what forms the clouds. As you move down the sky, the cream streaks left by the blue should be narrower and closer together, to give perspective.

3 Wait and watch for a couple of minutes and you'll see the clouds soften and become authentic-looking cirrus. Again, if there's a problem, it's almost certain to be that the blue is going in too wet, or that you've waited too long before putting it in.

◀ 2

◀ 3

▲ 1

▶ A quick vignette of
a cirrus sky.

131

▲ 1

Rain clouds

1 As before, put on your very pale Raw Sienna wash. However, this time it needs to be even wetter than it was before.

2 Mix up some good, rich Payne's Grey, with just enough Crimson Alizarin to warm it up (too much will make it pink). Load your hake with the mix and put in one large cloud across the top of the page. It is vital that your grey goes on darker than you think it should, as it will fade back considerably as it dries.

3 Move on down the page, producing smaller clouds, but allowing some of the original cream-coloured wash to show. Again, use a whole arm motion to do this. As you reach the horizon, remember to make the clouds narrower and closer together, so that they appear further away.

Now you must wait again for a couple of minutes while you watch your clouds move and soften. If you've got it right, you'll want to put up an umbrella!

▼ 2

▼ Some rapidly painted, dark rain clouds.

▲ 3

▲ 1   ▼ 2   ▲ 3

Evening sky

1 This sky is a little more complicated, but exciting and great fun to try. After the usual initial wash of Raw Sienna, put in a touch of blue at the top of the sky and graduate it to about a third of the way down.

2 Mix some Lemon Yellow and a little Crimson Alizarin and paint this across the bottom of the still wet Raw Sienna wash.

3 While your evening sky is softening, mix some very strong Payne's Grey and Crimson

Alizarin (a little more Alizarin than for the rain clouds). Now paint this in to form roughly sausage-shaped evening clouds, again remembering to make them smaller and closer together as you reach the horizon. As always, timing is critical and you have to work even faster than usual to make this sky look authentic.

▲ Practise doing quick little sky studies like this on scrap paper.

133

Composition and Design

Just as you wouldn't dream of building a house without an architect's plan, neither should you begin a painting without thinking it through first. The only materials that you need at this stage are a sketch pad and a soft pencil to try out some rough ideas for various compositions. I can't emphasize enough how important this pre-planning is – without it your painting simply won't progress in quality.

You can always tell when looking at a finished painting whether or not the artist is proficient in composition and design. No matter how beautifully applied the washes are or how well the colours are mixed, if a piece of work is poorly composed, it will never become a notable and satisfying painting. It will appear disjointed and lacking in harmony, and it won't invite the viewer into the scene. In other words, it simply won't 'gel'. It's very difficult to persuade my students that this pre-planning is worthwhile, but if you really want your paintings to improve – it is!

◀ Placing the horizon right across the centre is inclined to chop the picture into two halves, which is visually unsatisfying.

Placing the horizon

Perhaps the worst mistake you could make, especially when making sky paintings, is to place the horizon exactly in the centre of the paper. This immediately has the effect of chopping the painting in two. In most of the paintings featured in this section of the book, the horizon has been lowered to give more prominence to the sky itself. Obviously, if you want to give more dominance to the foreground, then you should move the horizon towards the top of the painting.

▼ Here the horizon is high with very little sky, just enough to show the mist on top of the hill. This gives more importance to the landscape features in the foreground.

▼ It is more usual to compose a sky painting with a low horizon. The area of land below the horizon simply provides a focal point and contrasting texture.

▶ **A Hilltop Town in Tuscany**
31 x 41 cm (12 x 16 in)
The focal point of this painting is the distant town with its sunlit church, deliberately contrasted against the dark sky behind.

The focal point

Another very important aspect to remember is that every picture needs a main point of interest, or focal point – an area or an object to which the eye is immediately drawn. This can be achieved in different ways. For example, the focal point could be the only man-made object in the painting, such as a boat or a house, no matter how small. Or it could be an animal or person. It might be the area of greatest contrast, such as the only white object against a dark background, or even the largest tree. As you look at the various illustrations throughout the book, you'll see what I mean.

There is a definite rule about positioning this main object of interest. Ideally, it should be at a different distance from each edge of the paper, and certainly never in the centre.

Leading the eye

The third point about composition is that you should make it as easy as possible for the viewer's eye to enter into your painting, and then to move around it to the main object of interest. Pathways, rivers, curving coastlines or shadows can all be used to achieve this. You might have noticed from the paintings of the great masters how adept they were in this aspect of composition. The Dutch painter Rembrandt (1606-69), for example, was highly skilled at leading the viewer's eye wherever he wanted to around his paintings.

▼ Here the eye is led into the picture by the track, taking the viewer to the barn – the main object of interest.

135

Design principles

Apart from being aware of the importance of good composition, you should also try to follow some basic rules of design, as these will greatly enhance your work. These rules are very straightforward and are largely a matter of common sense. The seven main principles of good design are listed below:

Unity, Contrast, Dominance, Variation, Balance, Harmony and Gradation.

You may not always need to include all seven principles in a single painting, but the more of them you adhere to, the more satisfactory will be the finished result. Take a look at each one separately in the examples that follow, thinking particularly about the ways in which they can be applied to skies.

Unity

A unified painting is one that is a harmonious whole, rather than a disjointed collection of objects. One way of achieving unity, which works particularly well in a sky painting, is to echo a tree or barn with a cloud shape . This also provides you with another aspect of unity, as the tree or barn unifies earth and sky, acting as a link between the two. A further unifying factor is to make some of the colours echo one another throughout the picture. In a sky painting, the most obvious way of doing this is to show the sky colour reflected in some water or mud below.

▲ The landscape and sky above are unified by showing the colours of the sky reflected in the water, while the trees link the two areas of the painting.

Contrast

Contrast, correctly applied in a painting, is a sure way to create excitement and interest. It is one of the principles that you will find easy to apply to every scene that you create. There are many ways of providing contrast. For example, you can contrast hard against soft with, perhaps, a church steeple silhouetted against soft cloud. For a contrast of tone, you might use a sunlit building set against a dark, threatening sky.

◀ The contrast is achieved here by placing the darkest parts of the picture – the rocks – immediately adjacent to the light areas. The dark clouds, too, contrast with the lighter areas of the sky, although not so strongly.

Dominance

This is largely a matter of common sense. When you are painting a sky, you should make one cloud larger or darker – in other words, more dominant – than the rest. Also, avoid dividing the sky equally between cloud and patches of blue. Give one area more importance than the other.

◀ The rich, dark green colour of the tree in the foreground ensures that this is the dominant part of the painting.

Variation

Variation is, as it sounds, a matter of avoiding monotony in repeated objects by changing their shape, size and colour. In a sky painting, this might be a matter of varying the cloud shapes and ensuring that the spaces between them are always different.

▶ Although these trees are positioned in a row and are of similar size, the colours are constantly changed to bring entertainment to the eye.

Balance

Although there are many different ways of balancing a painting, the most obvious and easiest example in a skyscape is to create a dark tone in the landscape, such as in a tree or building, to balance a dark cloud. The objects that balance each other should be different in size and be positioned obliquely.

▲ Informal balance is achieved by using the darker area of foreground rocks to balance the contrasted hut on the left of the scene.

▶ You'll notice here how the colours of the dominant cloud and the hillside on the right have been gradually changed to avoid boredom.

Harmony

Shapes and colours can both provide the harmonious elements needed in any painting. Think of similar circular and oval shapes, or a range of mauve and blue colours. A boulder in the foreground could perhaps be echoed by a cloud shape in the sky, while foreground shadows could be repeated in shape and colour in the sky above.

▲ The harmonizing effect in this peaceful little scene is brought about by the use of related colours. There are no strongly opposing colours.

Gradation

This principle is particularly important when you are portraying a large area of one colour, such as a cloudless blue sky. To avoid monotony, graduate the colour from a deep rich blue at the top to a cool cream on the horizon. Even in a completely overcast sky, take care to change the colour gradually, perhaps from palest grey to a deep, rich, thundercloud purple.

137

Perspective

Perspective is a word that strikes fear into the hearts of many an aspiring artist and yet, once tackled, it quickly becomes second nature. Your buildings will sit firmly on the ground, while trees and figures will recede into the distance as you narrow your roads.

So let me begin by explaining as simply as possible the basic facts about perspective. There are actually two kinds of perspective: linear and aerial. Linear perspective applies to skyscapes just as much as to landscapes, so let's look at this first.

Linear perspective

Put in its simplest form, the further away things are, the smaller they become. A good example of this is the effect you get when you look along a line of telegraph poles. Everyone can see and understand this, but then they often seem to forget it when they pick up their brushes and paints.

I find this particularly apparent when people are painting skies – many of my students paint all the clouds the same size, whether they are directly above them or right on the horizon. The resulting sky appears flat and uninteresting. All you need to do to avoid this is to apply the telegraph pole principle. You'll see immediately that the cloud above you must appear many times bigger than the cloud on the distant horizon.

Having mentioned the horizon, I must also add how vital this is to the whole question of perspective. As you look ahead of you, the horizon is at your eye level, and is where the lines of perspective meet at a 'vanishing point'. If you were looking along a railway track, this is where the two parallel lines of the rails would appear to meet.

Aerial perspective

Turning to aerial perspective, this is based on the basic principle of light tones appearing to recede into the distance, whereas darker tones seem to come forward. While aerial perspective will never be as apparent in skies

▲ This diagrammatic illustration shows how linear perspective applies to clouds just as much as to roads and telegraph poles.

as linear perspective, it could perhaps be applied by giving large, nearby clouds stronger tones and more contrast than those on the horizon.

Another important fact to remember is that objects appear to contain more blue the further away they are – in other words, they are cooler in colour. Nearby objects will always be richer and warmer.

When painting, it is always best to begin in the distance, gradually moving forward in planes to the foreground. What you should do is to start off in a whisper with pale, bluish colours, possibly applied wet-into-wet so that they are soft and out-of-focus. Then raise your voice with stronger, richer colours until you reach the foreground.

Greens in the countryside are a useful example. If you paint a distant tree or even a

meadow in too rich a green, you will immediately bring it forward. You need to reserve these rich greens for the foreground trees and vegetation.

▲ Evening on the Lake
31 x 41 cm (12 x 16 in)
Notice here the size of the clouds on the horizon compared with those at the top of the sky.

◀ Off the Norwegian Coast
20 x 20 cm (8 x 8 in)
The cool colours and light tones of the distant mountains are made to recede by using strong, rich colours and tones for the foreground rocks.

139

Working on Location

At first, it takes nerve to move outside to paint in the open air. You have to overcome the embarrassment of being watched and, to your own mind, being judged by the onlookers. However, working outside really is an essential part of your training as an artist, and your confidence will increase rapidly the more you try it. Apart from that, you'll soon learn that there is nothing like the excitement of setting down on paper the scene directly in front of you.

There are two options here. The first is simply to take out a small sketch pad and soft pencils and sketch your chosen scene. You can then take the sketch back to the studio to be translated into a painting later. As a beginner you may find that this is the less obtrusive option, as it doesn't attract curious onlookers. The second option is to set up your easel and watercolour materials and produce your whole picture on site.

▲ Two simple pencil sketches made with a 4B pencil in a spiral-bound cartridge pad. They can be used as references for paintings later on.

◄ Ron Ranson going out to paint on location with his folding metal easel and other essential equipment.

Making reference sketches

The most important point to remember when sketching is to use a whole range of tones, from white paper to solid black. Merely drawing outlines, or 'wire' as I call it, simply doesn't work, as this won't provide enough information to produce a watercolour painting back in the studio. You'll see what I mean from the sketches on this page.

Perhaps the best advice I can give you is to use only soft pencils – 2B to 6B. The most common pencils around, which are HB, won't produce a wide enough range of tones and are best kept just for writing.

140

Painting outdoors

While we have to accept that there are problems when painting outdoors, most of these can be overcome with a little foresight and planning. One important point is to keep your equipment simple. Don't weight yourself down with masses of materials. Instead, make a check-list of absolute necessities and then stick to it. This will also ensure that you take everything with you. There is nothing worse than finding the perfect spot to paint in, then discovering that you've no water, or have left your brushes or paints at home.

Be prepared for windy conditions. Keep some bull-dog clips with you to secure your paper to your board. With regard to the easel, the lightest probably isn't the best,

especially in wind. One way of holding your easel down is to tie some cord to it where the legs meet, and make a slip knot loop at the other end. All you need then is a weight, such as a large stone or log, to put into the loop to steady the easel. Having said that though, you can often find shelter from the wind behind a wall or building.

Direct sun can be a problem, too. Try to avoid the sun shining straight on to your paper. If you paint in such bright light, you will probably be disappointed with the washed-out appearance of your painting when you get it home.

A time to avoid, therefore, is midday, when the sun is immediately overhead. Before 10 a.m. and after 4 p.m., you'll find the light, as well as the shadows, more interesting.

▲ **An Evening Stroll**
29 x 38 cm (11½ x 15 in)
This simple scene was painted one evening on a beach in South Africa. The darkening sky is streaked with soft coral pink from the setting sun.

While on the subject of shadows, make sure you don't paint them in at different times as, over a two-hour period or so, their direction will change as the position of the sunlight alters. Wait until you've finished the rest of the painting and then put them in all at one time. In this respect, perhaps the easiest of conditions in which to paint is bright but overcast light, which will remain constant for many hours.

One type of weather condition you can do nothing about is rain, which can rapidly ruin a painting. At the first spot, turn your paper over and wait until the shower has passed. You can't fight rain with watercolour.

When you are looking for a good location to paint, take care to avoid trespassing. Always get permission before going on to private land, and be careful about closing gates and carrying your rubbish away with you. Artists are often regarded as rather special, so have a care and don't abuse the privilege.

When working in a town location, try to be as unobtrusive as possible, preferably not setting up your easel in the middle of a crowded pavement. However discreet you are, though, you'll inevitably be seen as a free show and find yourself the centre of attention. It is in situations like this that a sketchbook and camera are of great benefit.

▲ Shadows are most interesting when the sun is low in the sky. The shadows across the path in this painting help to define the surface.

◀ **Tuscan Hilltop Town**
31 x 38 cm (12 x 15 in)
I painted this scene quite quickly, sitting on a wall out of everyone's way, with a constant stream of buses starting and stopping in the immediate foreground. With this high horizon, the sky has a less important role, but still harmonizes with the rest of the painting.

▲ Here I'm enjoying myself painting on a beach in Oregon in the USA. The view in front of me when the photograph was taken is shown in the picture on the right.

▶ **Short Sands Beach, Oregon**
28 x 40 cm (11 x 15½ in)
The pale clouds are echoed by the highlights on the sea. The figures add a sense of scale.

Painting on holiday

There are many advantages in working with a group of like-minded people. For instance, it overcomes the anxiety of working alone, either in the countryside or in towns. Possibly one of the most enjoyable ways of joining a group is to go on an organized painting holiday, either at home or abroad. These are usually tutored and you'll find that you will make steady progress, as well as some good friends. Non-painting partners are usually welcomed.

This doesn't mean, however, that you can't paint on your own trips away. Paintings and sketches will give you a far livelier and more personal record of your adventures than any number of holiday snaps.

Taking reference photographs

Your cameras need to be light and compact if you wish to remain as unobtrusive as possible. It's important that you learn to compose your photographs properly, using the same rules of composition as you would in a painting. It's a strange phenomenon, but artists who spend time composing their paintings will forget entirely about design when looking through the viewfinder of a camera.

As a sky painter, it's a good idea to build up a large reference collection of various cloud formations to choose from when you are working on paintings in the future. You'll often get sky conditions which will disappear in seconds, but which can be captured on film and added to your reference library.

◀ Sitting on a fence taking photographs of an exciting sky.

143

Working in the Studio

As I said earlier, there is no substitute for working outdoors. However, working in the studio can bring its own rewards. Not only do you have more time to concentrate but there are also fewer distractions from sun, wind and rain. It's also an ideal time to experiment. You should never feel that you always have to produce a finished painting. Think of the experience rather than the end product, so that you are not held back by having set yourself a goal you must reach.

If it is at all possible, try to create a small space for yourself. You don't need a huge studio, but a 'painting space' in which you can leave your materials set out is invaluable.

Painting from references

Think about how you can make the best use of the reference material that you've gathered on location, both photographs and sketches.

Not that you should ever copy this material too literally; its purpose is to provide you with information and inspiration. Even though you may feel that you can produce a perfectly good sky out of your head, you will ensure authenticity by basing it roughly on a photograph. However, the finished painting will be your own individual interpretation of the scene, in which your memory of the atmosphere of the place will be aided by your references.

When you're working from reference material in the studio, speed is essential to maintain freshness but most of all to avoid overworking. The secret is to let a watercolour sky 'do its own thing' on a sloping surface. Don't push it around and play with it.

Try standing up for your sky painting, so that you have room for whole arm movements. This, combined with the use of the hake brush, will help you to produce fresh

▲ **Memories of Tuscany**
29 x 37 cm (11½ x 14½ in)
Having enjoyed running a workshop in Tuscany, I extended my enjoyment by painting this rural scene, with its important and busy sky, at home from memory.

yet strong skies, even though you are not working directly from the subject. Remember, too, that sky colour will always fade back when it dries, so give yourself a fright and use rich, strong colour. As one of my favourite artists, Ed Whitney, used to say, 'If it's right when it's wet, it's wrong when it's dry'.

Working from sketches

If you are working from sketches made on site, feel free to improve upon nature if necessary by moving objects around or by changing the heights of hills or mountains, for example. Look back to pages 134 to 137 to remind yourself of the principles of good composition and design.

The tonal sketches you made on location will be invaluable to remind you of the lights and darks in the original scene. Once again, you can enhance the tones or enrich the colours if you feel that this would improve the impact of the painting.

◀ This is the initial sketch I did on a recent visit to Scotland.

◀ Here, I've altered the lighting on the right of the middle distance to dramatize the sunlit shore. I've also darkened the tone of the right-hand foreground to balance the rich, dark cloud at top left.

◀ **Sunlight and Shadow**
28 x 35 cm (11 x 14 in)
In the finished painting, I wanted to create as much drama as possible by enriching the colour and deepening the tones. This type of lighting effect may only last for half a minute before it changes, hence the need for the sketches above.

145

▶ Photograph of a scene taken in California.

▲ Tonal sketch showing a change from a clear sky to cirrus clouds. Also, the horizon has been lowered.

◀ **Distant Sails, California**
31 x 40 cm (12 x 15½ in)
You can see in this finished painting how the sky has been made much more important, while the foreground has been minimized and simplified. The grasses have been used to balance the trees in the middle distance on the right.

Working from photographs

You may find, as you sort through your photographic references, that you have some beautiful landscapes with skies that look white and uninteresting. Don't necessarily blame yourself – it's just that the camera has got confused! An automatic camera will have worked out the exposure of the landscape, meaning that the much lighter sky will be overexposed and it will therefore look a bit bleached out. Conversely, if you are concentrating specifically on photographing the sky, the landscape beneath it will look too dark – underexposed, in fact.

Another problem to overcome when taking photographic references is that the beautiful scene in front of you may have a flat, overcast sky above it. On a different occasion, there might be a wonderful sky with nothing of much interest underneath it. The answer here is quite simple – mix and match.

You'll find on the opposite page an illustration of how an interesting sky from a different source can vastly improve a landscape painting. Do make sure, though,

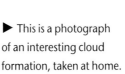
◀ I took this photograph on the Norfolk Broads. The sky is overcast and rather dull.

▶ This is a photograph of an interesting cloud formation, taken at home.

that your sky and landscape do actually match. This applies particularly to a scene with a lake or estuary in it – you will need to change the colour in the water to reflect the colour of the sky that you've decided to use.

Remember, when working from reference material, that you're not setting out to copy skies exactly from your photographs; in fact, it would be impossible to do so. Take from any photograph just the elements of the sky that you feel would be suitable for your painting – it may well be that you decide to use only a section, such as an interesting cloud formation.

▲ The tonal sketch shows how I have incorporated the two photographs into a single composition, using the curve of the cloud formation to echo the sweep of the river.

◀ **Horsey Mere**
29 x 38 cm (11½ x 15 in)
You'll see here how I have simplified the rather complex boats, making a lot of use of the white paper. Notice how the eye is taken round the curve of the river to the main object of interest – the windmill. The colour of the sky has been heightened to add more impact to the scene.

Creating Atmosphere

I have already mentioned briefly the impact that skies can have on the appearance and atmosphere of the landscape below them. In this chapter, you'll find some examples of this, including rather more extreme atmospheric effects, such as mist, snow, light shining through clouds, reflected sunlight and shadows. All these natural phenomena need different techniques if you are to depict them with authenticity. It's an exciting, challenging area, which will test your painting skill and will require plenty of practice. However, it will also bring you a lot of pleasure.

Mist

There is no medium that lends itself better to the portrayal of mist than watercolour. Consider first what mist actually is. The easiest way to explain it is as a cloud on the ground, consisting of fine particles of water which form a series of 'veils'. If you study J.M.W. Turner's (1775–1851) portrayal of misty scenes, you'll notice that they are always full of subtle and restrained colour, never just grey. Think of a landscape in the early

morning, when the sun is just beginning to break through the mist – the whole scene would be bathed in various golden tones.

In any misty scene, the tones are flattened and you'll be painting silhouettes with very little detail. However, you will need a strong foreground interest to emphasize the effect of the mist. Not everything in the painting should appear woolly and soft.

Perhaps the best way to begin this type of scene is to wet the whole surface of the paper and then work from the distance to the foreground, gradually increasing the strength

▲ In these two paintings you can see the difference in atmosphere created by the different sky conditions behind the windmill.

◀ **Morning Mist on the Coast of Maine**
25 x 33 cm (10 x 13 in)
This scene shows the rolling ground mist that is so prevalent on this coast. After putting in the tops of the trees in relatively strong colour, the bottom part of the trees was softened by using clear water.

of your paint for each plane. You'll find that when you reach the foreground, the paper will be almost dry, so that your image will be crisper and stronger – just as it should be.

Shadows

When scattered clouds pass over a landscape, particularly over hills, they produce attractive patterns of light and shade, which can be helpful in indicating the profile of the scenery below. Shadows also add excitement and variety to a scene.

Snow

Snow scenes are possibly the most attractive to any artist and are a joy to paint. However, you'll need to handle them with discretion. Do remember that snow on the ground is never universally white because, although the effects are more subtle than with water, it does to a certain extent reflect the sky above the snowy landscape. Keep this in mind and you'll find that your snow scenes will soon improve dramatically.

Shadows are even more important in snowy landscapes than they are usually, as they show the profile of the ground in the absence of other features. They also present a wonderful opportunity to use subtle mixes of blues and mauves.

Creating falling snow requires a little experimentation, but can be great fun to do. Take an old toothbrush and load it with some opaque white gouache. Then rub a pencil or the handle of a paint brush towards you across the top of the toothbrush. The paint will spatter on to the paper and can look very pleasing. Don't over do the spattering though – as with so many other aspects of creating atmosphere, subtlety is all.

▼ **Winter Dawn**
28 x 38 cm (11 x 15 in)
This painting shows how you can give the impression of falling snow by spatttering white gouache from a toothbrush.

149

Sun through clouds

A fascinating and popular effect to attempt is depicting the rays of the sun coming from behind clouds. Here, it isn't the application of paint that's important, but the removal of it from a completely dry painting. To achieve this, use an eraser to rub away lines of paint from the area beneath the clouds, remembering that the rays are not parallel, but radiate out from the hidden sun.

Experiment with different erasers for different effects. Softest of all is a putty eraser, then an ordinary pencil eraser. The hardest is an ink eraser. The paper on which you are working makes a difference, too. Bockingford watercolour paper, in particular, is very responsive to this technique.

▲ **Silver Rays**
29 x 38 cm (11½ x 15 in)
Here, enough paint was removed with a soft eraser to depict the sun's rays shining on to the ground. Notice how the rays radiate outwards from the cloud-covered sun.

Don't be too firm with watercolour. Give it freedom to express itself.

Sparkle on water

The ideal brush to create light sparkling on water is the hake, and the secret is lightness of touch and speed of stroke. This technique is most satisfactory when used on Not or rough paper. What you're aiming to do is just touch the high points of the paper with the brush, leaving the indents free of paint. It is the white paper which produces the apparent sparkle. Get yourself a pile of scrap paper and try this over and over again.

Sunsets

There is no doubt that evening skies provide some of the most beautiful effects to be seen in nature. However, sunsets need to be tackled with discretion. No matter how gaudy the actual sky appears, it simply will not look believable in a painting. Remember that you or someone else may be looking at the picture for many years to come, and gaudiness soon palls.

Mixing various combinations of Crimson Alizarin and Lemon Yellow wet-into-wet near the horizon is very effective in suggesting a sky at sunset, and you'll see this illustrated here. Possibly the most important rule is to put in all the subtle colour variations in the sky before indicating the cloud formations on top, in stronger colour.

Sunsets can be at their most effective when they are combined with water or snow. The reflected sky colours will provide both harmony and unity in any scene.

▲ **A Morning Sail**
23 x 31 cm (9 x 12 in)
The secret of creating sparkle on the surface of water is to work quickly and lightly, preferably with a hake brush.

◀ **Severn Estuary at Sunset**
23 x 33 cm (9 x 13 in)
I first painted a graduated wash on the sky, adding a mixture of Crimson Alizarin and Lemon Yellow at the bottom. Later I put in the clouds, made up of Payne's Grey and Crimson Alizarin. The sky colour also appears in the landscape below.

151

Skies and Water

◀ **Misty Morning on Williamette River, Oregon**
29 x 38 cm (11½ x 15 in)
Painting a wet-into-wet scene like this one, in which the sky and scenery are reflected in still water, is great fun. Make sure that the reflections, though softer than the surroundings and objects such as the boat, are about the same shape and tone.

If painting skies can be an exciting and fulfilling exercise, then combining them with areas of water can be doubly so. What's more, there is plenty of water around – after all, about seven-tenths of the surface of the earth is covered by it.

However, if water doubles the excitement, it can also double the challenge to the artist, especially as its character can vary from a still pond or lake to a fast-flowing stream or foam-flecked sea. Still water can act as a mirror, giving an almost perfect reflection of the sky and everything above it, whereas moving water, with its very different mood, has its own special requirements.

Still water

Being without colour itself, water will reflect the forms and colours around it beautifully. If there is nothing else around it, then the water will reflect the sky. When you repeat the sky colours in the water, you will be creating harmony in your painting, as the blues, greys, mauves, or even pinks and yellows of the sky are echoed in the water below.

Even if the sky is all one colour, don't forget that you must graduate the wash you lay down for the water, just as you have for the sky. The water in the foreground should be darker, getting lighter as it reaches the horizon.

▲ Highland Stream
25 x 35 cm (10 x 14 in)
My objective here was to create the illusion of rapid movement in the water. You can see how much paper was left white while the paint was put on with very fast strokes in the direction of the water flow.

Moving water

Moving water requires a completely different painting technique. To indicate areas of foam and spray, you'll need to leave a lot of the white paper untouched (see page 151). The strokes that you do put in must be worked quickly, following the direction of the water flow. Fast-moving water will give back very little in the way of reflections, except for the basic surrounding colour.

Reflections

Reflections are a wonderful way of bringing unity into your painting, as they repeat the colours and shapes of surrounding objects, such as buildings, trees or posts. Remember that if an object is situated right at the edge of the water, the reflection will be the same size, but if it is further back the reflection will be shortened.

To depict reflections in an expanse of still water, begin by painting the water itself, using horizontal strokes to put in a graduated wash of the main colour used for the sky. You'll find that the hake is an ideal brush for this. While this first wash is still quite damp, put in the reflections with vertical strokes, compensating for the water already on the paper by using rich paint. The reflections will soften a little due to the water content of the paper, but because of the rich paint, the basic colour and shape will remain true to the reflected object.

▶ Tranquil Evening
23 x 31 cm (9 x 12 in)
After painting in the sky, I first indicated the river by using the sky colour above it, and then added the reflections of the trees while the first wash was still wet. Notice how the dark cloud and the group of trees balance each other.

153

Completing the Painting

Every sky painting needs a foreground, however minimal, to give it scale and impact. But it is important that the two parts of the picture are completely integrated to provide unity between them. You can achieve this in several ways – by repeating the sky colours in parts of the landscape; by linking the land to the sky by placing a vertical element on the horizon, rather like a piece in a jigsaw puzzle; or by echoing the shape of one object with another, perhaps a rounded cumulus cloud with a tree. The shadows of racing clouds on the ground can provide

another effective link between the upper and lower areas of a painting.

Generally, when you are working on a sky painting, you have only got about 5 cm (2 in) of space at the bottom of the paper to convey a landscape that in reality goes back for miles. So you'll need to exploit your knowledge of aerial perspective to the utmost (see page 138). For example, you could put in distant hills with a flat grey-blue shade, warming up the colours gradually as you move towards the front of the painting and confining any textural details to the foreground.

▼ **Late Afternoon, Norfolk Broads**
29 x 38 cm (11½ x 15 in)
The closest trees, which link the land to the sky, were painted with a rigger and some dry brush work with a hake. The ground is mainly a warm mix of Light Red and Raw Sienna, and the water contains the same colours as the sky to provide unity.

Texture in the foreground

One of the main mistakes to avoid in your watercolours is to ruin a lovely fresh sky, which of necessity must be painted quickly and courageously, by producing a muddy, overworked landscape below it. Tall grasses and reeds are probably the most commonly used, and overworked, foreground subjects, whether the scene is a grassy field, a river bank or a forest floor. However, these seemingly impossible masses of vegetation can easily be symbolized. Rocky ground, too, can be suggested with just a few brush marks.

For instance, take woodland undergrowth, a grassy field or some rocky ground that starts at your feet and goes back into the distance. Much of this can be left plain and uncluttered. All the real textures can be confined to the absolute foreground, quickly disappearing to almost nothing as the ground recedes.

To create a grassy foreground texture, lay down an overall wash first and then, with a rigger, put in a few blades of grass to reach about halfway back to the horizon. These will soften and become out of focus. As the paint becomes slightly less damp, indicate a few light blades of grass with your fingernail. Finally, use a corner of the hake with some rich paint to suggest some more foreground features, such as small stones or rocks.

▲ **The Mauve Hills**
31 x 41 cm (12 x 16 in)
To create texture, a dry brush technique was used on top of the initial colour wash after it had dried.

▼ Grasses, stones and rocks are useful for creating textural interest in the foreground of a landscape, but make sure that you paint them simply and economically. Just a few brush strokes can symbolize a mass of different features.

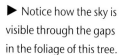

▲ These rocks are given a convincing solid form by using a light tone on the tops and dark shading on the sides.

▶ Notice how the sky is visible through the gaps in the foliage of this tree.

Specific landscape features

Large foreground rocks often feature in country landscapes, so the ability to portray them authentically and with simplicity is essential. The secret is to make them look as solid and heavy as possible. Remember that the top of a rock, as it faces the sky, will be much lighter than the sides, which are in shadow and are therefore darker. By painting rocks in this way, you will give a convincing impression of their heaviness and solidity.

Trees, too, are a prominent feature of many landscapes, and will help you to connect and unify the sky with the land in your painting. When you paint a tree over the sky, leave plenty of gaps in the foliage, otherwise it will tend to look like a toffee apple – and the birds need a way through! Another tip: don't leave a space in your initial sky wash to anticipate a tree to be put in later – you will always need the sky colour to show through.

▼ This scene shows trees at three different distances. The background hill, although completely wooded, is treated as a flat colour. The trees in the middle distance are very loosely indicated and only the foreground trees are given some detail.

▲ Nearby trees always appear stronger and richer than more distant ones. You'll see that the tree on the far left, being further away, is cooler and flatter than the large one in the foreground.

Buildings

There will be times when your skyscapes will benefit from simple buildings beneath them. For instance, a sharp-edged barn could be used to balance a heavy cloud on the other side of a painting. A 25 mm (1 in) flat brush is excellent for indicating simple roofs with an economy of stroke.

A useful device for creating a main object of interest in a landscape is to set a white house against a dark tree. Painting a church tower with a few roofs around it is a perfect way to indicate a village. Boatyards and yacht basins, too, provide distinctive features in skyscapes. All that is required to indicate a mast in the distance is a single touch of the 25 mm (1 in) flat.

Don't be afraid of buildings. The more economically they are painted, the better they look, and their sharp edges act as a good foil to the softness of the sky.

▲ **On the Island of Hydra**
18 x 25 cm (7 x 10 in)
The roof tiles on this Greek house are indicated with the edge of a flat brush. The distant village is put in with even more economy.

▶ Here you can see how buildings can be added to a landscape to create foreground interest. These houses were painted very simply, using a 25 mm (1 in) flat brush.

DEMONSTRATION EIGHT

River Valley

This favourite site is very near my home and I'm unlikely to be disturbed while painting on the river bank. The hills on both sides are covered with trees, so the scene changes dramatically with the seasons of the year. In this summer view, the landscape is set against a cloudless blue sky.

▶ First stage

Colours

French Ultramarine

Lemon Yellow

Raw Sienna

Light Red

Burnt Umber

Payne's Grey

First Stage

For this painting, I chose a 300 gsm (140 lb) Bockingford paper with a Not surface. First, I outlined the scene using a 3B pencil. Then I put a very pale wash of Raw Sienna over the sky area with my hake brush. While this was still wet, I made up a rich wash of French Ultramarine. Using a whole arm movement and moving backwards and forwards across the top of the sky, I gradually worked down towards the horizon with the Ultramarine, reducing pressure until the brush was just touching the paper at the horizon. With the paper tilted at an angle of 45 degrees, this produced a graduated wash.

When the sky was dry, I began on the hills. Using a mixture of Ultramarine and Lemon

Yellow, I painted in the whole hillside. I then blended a strong mixture of Lemon Yellow and Ultramarine into the right-hand hillside to bring this area forward. While this was still wet, I mixed a very strong Payne's Grey and Lemon Yellow and painted a line of trees in front of the hill, using a corner of my hake.

Second Stage

With a mixture containing Lemon Yellow and just a touch of Ultramarine, and using the hake horizontally, I put in the right-hand field. Next came the river bank itself. I used diagonal strokes to portray its slope, adding touches of Light Red and Raw Sienna with darker accents made from a mixture of Ultramarine and Burnt Umber. Moving

▲ Second stage

across to the left-hand trees, I painted these with a corner of my hake, using Payne's Grey and Lemon Yellow.

For the river, I put on a very wet wash of Ultramarine. Then, making up a strong, rich mixture of Payne's Grey and Lemon Yellow, I dropped in the reflection of the hillside on the right and the tree on the left, making sure that the reflections were not too anaemic.

Finished Stage

While the river was still damp, I wiped out two white streaks on the water with a dry hake brush (see page 125) to indicate a wind-ruffled patch of water. Once those were in place, I then concentrated on creating the foreground on the left-hand side.

I painted the bank in the foreground in a mix of Raw Sienna and Ultramarine to bring it forward. Finally, I put in the large tree on the left and the foliage on the river bank below it with a rich mixture of Lemon Yellow and Ultramarine.

▼ **River Valley**
25 x 35 cm (10 x 14 in)

The Road to a Village

One of the most fascinating but challenging cloud types to paint is cumulus. Remember that these are like fluffy pieces of cotton wool with a spotlight shining on to one side. One foreground cloud should dominate, and the rest should rapidly decrease in size as they move towards the horizon. Bear in mind that the blue you put on for the sky must create negative shapes for the clouds.

▶ First stage

Colours

French Ultramarine

Raw Sienna

Light Red

Burnt Umber

Payne's Grey

Crimson Alizarin

First Stage

Again, I chose some Bockingford 300 gsm (140 lb) Not paper for this demonstration. I indicated the hills, road and houses with a 3B pencil.

Mixing a very weak solution of Raw Sienna, I covered the whole sky with a wash, using a hake. I then made up a wash of rich French Ultramarine. While the Raw Sienna was still damp, I painted in the blue sky, leaving the cumulus clouds as negative shapes in the original cream and making sure that the blue became slightly paler towards the horizon. Then I very quickly mixed up Payne's Grey and Crimson Alizarin in order to put it on before the original Raw Sienna had dried. This darker colour had to be painted lightly on to the right-hand side of each cloud to give the illusion of sunshine on the left-hand side. When you try this yourself, you may find that it takes four or five attempts before you produce a credible cumulus sky, so work on scrap paper to begin with.

Second Stage

After putting in the distant hills with a mixture of Ultramarine and Light Red, it was time to paint in the village houses. These were done almost entirely with the 25 mm (1 in) flat brush, which is ideal for simplifying buildings, walls and gates, even church spires. The windows, too, were indicated with a touch of this flat brush. I only used the hake to paint the trees in between the houses. To prevent boredom, I varied the colours in the village, leaving plenty of untouched white paper for the gable ends and other light areas. The roofs are a mixture of Light Red and Raw Sienna.

Third Stage

I now wanted to create an entry into the picture that would take the eye into the village itself. The perspective on the road is slightly exaggerated, which always helps to lead the viewer's eye into a painting. I aimed to introduce several colours and textures into the foreground area to add interest. After indicating the flat areas with horizontal strokes of the hake, using a thin mix of Raw Sienna and Ultramarine, I worked with the corner of the hake and various thicker mixes of Raw Sienna, Light Red, Burnt Umber and Ultramarine to produce bushes.

161

▶ **The Road to a Village**
31 x 41 cm (12 x 16 in)

Finished Stage

I felt that the picture would be made more exciting by looking from foreground shadow into a sunny field before reaching the village. The shadows were caused by trees on the right, just out of the picture. The shadow colour was made up of Light Red and Ultramarine, and I put this in with a quick, light sweep of the hake, using a whole arm movement. I left one or two sunny streaks among the shadows. Finally, I added fine grasses in the foreground with the rigger, using the same mixes as for the bushes in the previous stage.

▶ Detail of finished
painting

Sunset on the Estuary

This river estuary is another favourite painting spot within a short distance of my home. The best time to paint there is at low tide, when the sky is reflected off the wet sand. The pink and yellow colours of the sunset and the grey streaks of the clouds make this a very dramatic picture, especially with the dark silhouettes of the moored yacht and the posts in the foreground.

Colours

Raw Sienna

Burnt Umber

French Ultramarine

Lemon Yellow

Crimson Alizarin

Payne's Grey

◀ First stage

First Stage

After establishing a flat pencil horizon on a piece of Bockingford 300 gsm (140 lb) Not paper, I indicated the moored yacht on the right. Using a hake, I painted a very pale Raw Sienna wash over the whole sky area. I then put in a graduated wash of Ultramarine from the top and, quickly washing out my brush, painted a strip of Lemon Yellow two-thirds of the way down. Adding Crimson Alizarin to this wash, I painted the bottom of the sky. If you do all this while the original Raw Sienna wash is still wet, all the colours will blend as they have here.

Second Stage

Next I tackled the clouds. For these, I had to use thicker paint in a blend of Payne's Grey and Crimson Alizarin. There was no time to be hesitant – I had to put them in boldly and quickly, using my whole arm to make these strokes across the paper. The fact that the sky wash was still slightly damp meant that the clouds softened and blended.

◀ Second stage

▲ Third stage

Third Stage

When the sky was dry, I painted in the land on the horizon with a mixture of Payne's Grey and Crimson Alizarin. Once this had dried, I rendered the water of the estuary in Lemon Yellow, Crimson Alizarin and Ultramarine.

My aim here was to mirror the sky as much as possible. When this, too, was dry, I put in the rocks and beach. I varied the mix here with Ultramarine, Burnt Umber and Raw Sienna, using the dry brush technique (see page 124) with the edge of the hake to provide texture.

Finished Stage

I added the various posts on the left and in the centre, as well as painting the moored yacht – this wasn't actually in the scene in front of me, but became the focal point of the whole picture. These details were put in with a mix of Burnt Umber and Ultramarine, using a 25 mm (1 in) flat brush.

▶ **Sunset on the Estuary**
31 x 41 cm (12 x 16 in)

▲ Detail of finished painting

166

Vibrant Watercolours
By Hazel Soan

Imagine mouthwatering colours skimming across the textured white paper, with deep mysterious darks dissolving softly into radiant lights. Vibrant watercolours are those that sing out from the page. They make you feel good, they seduce you with their bold impact and wonderful techniques. They are a delight to behold and a joy for the artist to paint.

How do you paint vibrant watercolours? How do you prevent your paintings from becoming lacklustre or overworked? The secret is in knowing what watercolour can do, and having the confidence to use that knowledge. The best way to gain confidence is to practise, but few people actually have enough spare time to do so. I aim to show you how to short cut your practice time and suggest ways in which you can make your own paintings vibrant.

The right approach

When you are learning to use watercolours you can sometimes try so hard that your paintings are filled with frustration and overworking, losing their liveliness. However, there are aids to follow that will help you make your paintings vibrant. By choosing a subject you really like and are

▲ **This is My Town**
43 x 56 cm (17 x 22 in)
Watercolour, with its rainbow of pigments, its spontaneous brushwork and the immediacy of its translucent washes, is the perfect medium for creating lively, animated paintings.

interested in, allowing yourself to be relaxed about the painting process, and genuinely enjoying mixing and laying those delicious colours, there is every chance that you can create a successful watercolour. Look hard before starting to paint, examine the subject as if seeing it for the first time, and put aside any preconceptions of how you think something must look.

What is your goal?

Most beginners are only too happy to achieve some form of likeness to their chosen subject. But this, though admirable, is not your only goal, You want to paint something with that little bit extra, a

painting that goes beyond straight reproduction. Perhaps what really attracts you to paint a subject is actually not the subject itself, but the way the light falls upon it, or the arrangement of shapes. That attraction or inspiration is what you want your painting to be about.

Striking a chord

Sometimes when you strike a slightly off-beat chord visually you create a watercolour that is vibrant. Even a mundane object like a pair of old boots can make an exciting painting. If you approach an age-old theme in a refreshingly different way the viewer is jolted into a response, momentarily seeing with your eyes and feeling your passion.

When something is understated, or slightly ambiguous, it often attracts attention; in order to see it clearly the viewer has to get involved, and is consequently drawn into the picture.

Know-how

Technical ability is not a prerequisite for a vibrant watercolour. However, becoming familiar with colours and tones and learning to apply paint effectively to paper will help you to express your interest in the subject with confidence, and enable you to achieve the lively, vibrant watercolours you seek. Learn the main watercolour techniques and give special attention to brush strokes and laying paint as well as examining the thought behind the painting.

Step-by-step demonstrations guide you through the process of building up a vibrant watercolour, and encourage you to convey your inspiration and passion in vibrant watercolours of your own. Here is a world longing to be explored. Have fun!

▼ **Decked in Scarlet**
76 x 56 cm (30 x 22 in)
One of the most exciting qualities of watercolour is its power to suggest detail without actually painting it. Wet-in-wet washes can create ambiguity, brush strokes create energy, and an understated approach draws the viewer into the painting.

169

Watercolour Techniques

The radiance and spontaneity of watercolour paint are two of its most attractive qualities. To make the most of these you will need to know how to mix and lay your colours. Mastery of technique will not guarantee vibrant paintings, but it will give your watercolours a chance to show you what they can do and you a chance to express yourself more succinctly.

Just add water

To release the wonderful pigments in watercolour paint you must dilute them with water. Not only do they become lighter in colour the more water you use, but they also often look very different in colour from their solid form. How much water to use is only gained by practice. Beginners often make their colours too wishy-washy or use them too thick, so that either a general dullness prevails or the painting is garish.

To load your brush with water for mixing, dip the whole body of the brush into clean water and as you lift it out roll it against the edge of the water jar to shape the point and remove some of the water.

If you want drier or more intense colour dab the water off the brush on a piece of kitchen paper before you touch the palette, turning the brush sideways on the paper in a fashion that keeps its tip pointed.

Translucence

Watercolour is a transparent medium that gains its radiance from light bouncing back from the white paper through the layers of thin colour on top. Watercolour paintings are made up of successive tints of colour, but if you paint too many layers on top of each other you will reduce or lose that

transparency. Examine vibrant watercolours and you will find in them a minimum of overpainting. Make each layer count; it must be there for a reason. One or two rich washes will preserve radiance, whereas lots of layers will tend to dull a colour down.

◀ To mix a pale colour place the brush on to the pan of pigment and rub it with the tip of the brush only, to release the colour. Place this on the palette to check its strength and gather more from the pan until you have enough for the passage of painting involved.

◀ For larger, richer pools of colour twist the body of the brush in the pan, lifting the colour into the hairs of the brush. Lay this on the palette and keep adding from the pan until you have enough.

◀ The colours from tubes yield up their pigment far more readily than pans as they are already semi-liquid. Squeeze a little paint on to the palette. Take a little pigment, add water, then add a little more pigment until you reach the colour you desire.

Brush strokes

The initial brush strokes over virgin paper carry a vitality that overpainting may obscure. Paint with boldness, laying down your colours in shapes that are meaningful rather than indiscriminate. The joy of watercolour painting is that you build up an image with areas of colour rather than outlines. The brush stroke itself has a power of description, so harness that characteristic to create evocative paintings.

Take time to mix the right strength of colour before you add the brush stroke to your painting. Testing colours on the painting and adding layers and layers of hopeful washes to strengthen a colour is a

▲ Each brush stroke is laid down quickly in a mark that describes the shapes within the flower.

► The body of the tomato is just one broad circular-shaped brush stroke of Cadmium Red. While still wet more red is touched into the left-hand side, immediately suggesting three-dimensional form.

▲ To suggest a treeline different greens and browns are dabbed into the base of the wet sky wash and allowed to spread.

recipe for disaster. The lovely broken edge of a first wash as it caresses the tooth of the paper will be lost underneath successive brush strokes and the life of the painting will be gone for ever.

Most said with minimum means

Imagine you are allowed only 50 brush strokes per painting. You would take care to get each one right. You would make sure each time you laid your brush down that it carried the desired colour to the chosen place and made the required shape – no dithering with meaningless brush marks or insipid layers of colour. You would spend more time mixing in the palette and more time looking at the subject. In a successful watercolour more time is spent off the paper than on it. A painting's success is no less deserved because it is arrived at quickly.

▲ The silhouette of the tree is created with the tip of a fully loaded round brush in one continual wash without seams.

▲ A blue wash is painted in shapes equivalent to the shadows on the boy. Burnt Sienna is then laid in brush strokes that colour the skin and dark areas of clothes.

◄ The dry-brush strokes on the bark follow the shape of the tree to suggest its form.

▲ To paint wet-in-wet prepare the colours in sufficient quantities first. Touching in the second colour at the right moment takes practice. If the first colour is too wet the second will run quickly into it, but the longer you wait the more slowly it spreads.

Painting techniques

There are two main techniques for applying watercolour to paper, and in general you will use a combination of the two: wet-in-wet and wet-on-dry.

Wet-in-wet

The technique of allowing one colour to run into another while it is still wet is called wet-in-wet. As the colours merge they create gentle grading and soft evocative effects. If lots of water and pigment are used dynamic explosions of colour occur as backruns push pigment into unpredictable patterns.

Atmospheric washes

You can dampen the whole, or parts, of the paper with clear water and then run your colour into this to create soft atmospheric washes – for hazy skies, for instance. Mix a good quantity of colour, use a large brush and lay the colour across the dampened page in successive slightly overlapping washes. If you want the wash to be paler at the bottom gradually dilute the mix as you go. Tilt the

▶ **Walking the Dog**
28 x 36 cm (11 x 14 in)
A variegated wash occurs if you lay several colours onto the wetted paper. This thundery sky results from Yellow Ochre, Burnt Sienna, Sepia, Prussian Blue and Indigo intermingling on the wet paper.

paper to encourage an even flow, and do not be tempted to fiddle with any perceived imperfections in the wash as it is drying.

Wet-on-dry

Radiant, lively watercolours are created with this method. The watercolour is painted on to the dry paper and allowed to dry completely before successive layers of colour are laid on top. The overlapping washes are crisp edged and glowing, especially if some of the previous colour is left untouched by the colour laid next. Uneven pooling of the colour as it dries can add to its charm, so avoid the temptation to 'perfect' the wash. Leave it to dry unmolested.

Using both techniques

You can combine both techniques in any watercolour painting. You can also lay a wet-in-wet wash over a dried wash by wetting it slightly with clear water. Brush the second colour on so that it blends into the wet area over the first colour. Always wet the paper well beyond the area you wish the paint to spread, or you will end up with a hard edge where the paint meets the edge of the water. Make sure the wash underneath is completely dry before you rewet it or you will disturb it and ruin its quality.

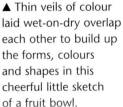

▲ Thin veils of colour laid wet-on-dry overlap each other to build up the forms, colours and shapes in this cheerful little sketch of a fruit bowl.

◀ **Grantchester Meadows**
28 x 36 cm (11 x 14 in)
To create soft foliage the paper is damped with clear water over the dried underwash of pale geen. Darker green is brushed on wet-in-wet and spreads softly into the damped area. Wet-on-dry brush strokes create contrasting crisp marks.

▶ Fine hairy lines can be created by actually splaying the hairs of the brush apart after loading with paint. To create the grasses I dragged a splayed round brush upward across the paper to release the paint. For the birch bark I used a flat brush and took the splayed stroke around the trees to help shape the trunks.

Dry-brush

The ragged edge of the dry-brush stroke is a marvellous counterfoil to the soft edges of wet-in-wet colour. To make dry-brush

marks tap off all excess moisture from your brush on the rag and mix your paint with very little water. On a rough paper, the brush stroke will create a delightful and often dramatic broken edge as it scumbles over the tooth of the paper.

Reserving white paper

Despite the fact that watercolour paper is seldom bright white, the highlights and lightest lights you can obtain in watercolour are nearly always created by leaving the white paper unpainted.

The freshest method of reserving the white paper is simply to avoid painting over it by careful observation or around a drawn guideline. The slightly irregular shapes left between passages of paint are another of the most appealing characteristics of watercolour. Take note of the lightest parts of your painting, and leave them as white paper from the start and throughout the painting. If, later on, you wish to tint them, then nothing is lost.

▶ **Kensington Gardens**
13 x 18 cm (5 x 7 in)
Looking into the light creates haloes around lit objects backed by a dark background. What better way to create this light in a painting than by leaving areas of white paper between the highlit figures and the background of foliage?

from a wet wash, or for an immediate correction. Once the wash is dry it is still possible to lift off the colour to some or almost all the extent by rubbing the required area gently with a damp brush or sponge and dabbing off the loosened pigment.

White paint

White gouache can be used for retrieving small highlights, and you might find it easier on occasion than trying to paint round tiny areas or lines of white paper. Colour can also be added to the gouache to create a tinted light if you wish.

A thin wash of white will make a colour look less vivid. Paint a dilute wash across the colour like a veil and then leave it to dry without touching it.

▲ Masking fluid was used to protect the blades of corn from the variegated wash. The unmasked shapes are apt to look blobby unless they are quite carefully painted with attention to their shape. After the masking is removed the stalks are touched in with pale Yellow Ochre.

Masking fluid is an oft-used timesaver for protecting the white paper during the painting process. It is a latex fluid, which is resistant to water. Paint it on at the start over details that you wish to keep white, and rub it off when the paint is dry to reveal untouched white paper.

Lifting out

While watercolour is wet it is possible to dab it off almost without stain. You can use this technique for retrieving highlights

▲ A size 4 brush with a fine tip and neat moist white gouache enables you to paint the detail of railings over a dark background.

▶ The bright orange wash is painted on to wet paper and the sun and its reflection are lifted off immediately with a piece of kitchen roll. The colour is then dragged across the path of the sun from either side to create gentle ripples.

175

Confident Colour

Colour has a predominant part to play in creating vibrant watercolours. Not only do individual colours affect other colours, but particular colours provoke different reactions in the viewer. The groupings of similar or opposite colours can also evoke a specific mood or atmosphere in a painting. Exploiting the properties of colour will help you create striking pictures.

Colour theory certainly helps in the understanding of how to use colour, but, as with everything in painting, it is practice that counts. I find it better to experiment in actual paintings than with colour swatches.

◄ **Venetian Corners**
76 x 56 cm (30 x 22 in)
This watercolour is full of colour, and yet the palette consists of just six colours, a warm and cool version of the three primaries: Cadmium Red and Crimson Alizarin, Yellow Ochre and Aureolin, Cobalt Blue and Prussian Blue.

Basic colours

In painting red, yellow and blue are called primary colours because all other colours can be made from mixing two or three of them together. Secondary colours are so called because they are the colours we obtain from mixing just two of the primary colours together. Thus red and yellow make orange, blue and yellow make green, and red and blue make purple.

Interaction of colour

No colour is absolute. Colours change under different lights and against different hues and tones. Colours juxtaposed can enhance or detract from each other. A red next to a green or turquoise will vibrate with excitement. Put a blue next to an orange and both colours will look brighter. Mauve and yellow, when placed adjacent, will make the other colour appear stronger.

What is the reason for this interaction? Each of the pairs of colours mentioned includes a primary and a secondary colour, which, if both were mixed together, would then include all three primary colours. These paired combinations are called opposite colours because each is as different from the other as a colour can be. They are also called complementary colours because together they comprise the three primaries. The artist can make use of these properties to help the colours stand out or to mute any colours that are too bright.

When you mix the three primaries together you can make any number of browns, greys, and ultimately blacks. It follows, therefore, that if two opposite colours are mixed together they will also make those greys, browns and blacks.

▼ **Crossing the Kalahari**
43 x 76 cm (17 x 30 in)
The contrasting complementary colours of blue and orange are used to dynamic effect in this painting of gemsbok crossing the harsh stark dunes of the Kalahari desert.

Warm and cool colours

Another vital ingredient for the watercolour artist to understand is the 'temperature' of the colours one uses.

For instance, if you wish to evoke a cool atmosphere, then use more blue colours in your painting. However, if you want to create warmth and excitement, you must play with reds and oranges.

This warmth or coolness is relative. Each colour that is not a pure primary leans towards another; thus Crimson Alizarin is a red, but it is a purple-red and veers toward blue. It is, therefore, a cool red even though it is a warm colour in relation to blue.

By mixing colours of like temperature you can create colours that are more vivid than if you mix a warm and a cool colour together. To make bright colours, therefore, you should always mix two together that have the same temperature; for example, Cadmium Red and Cadmium Yellow. For duller colours, try mixing two of different temperatures; for example, French Ultramarine and Yellow Ochre.

Seeing colour

When you look at an object or a landscape, never presume that you already know the colour. Nothing remains the same as the light upon it changes. A white wall may glow rose with the reflected light from terracotta tiles, or turn blue as it is cast in shadow.

Watercolour lends itself to the exaggeration of reflected colour. Its gentle tints and overlaying washes can warm up or cool down any passage of colour at a stroke. As you look more closely you will notice colours that you did not expect to be there. That alone is an exciting discovery, and then to be able to emulate those colours with paint is an inspiration in itself.

If you remember that you are playing with tints rather than opaque colour, then

▲ **Umbrella against the Sun**
15 x 20 cm (6 x 8 in)
▶ **In the Stillness**
25 x 36 cm (10 x 14 in)
By comparing these two paintings of African trees you can see the warmth that red confers on a painting and the cool calm effect brought by blue.

◀ The lemon, brightly lit, reflects some of its own colour on to the cloth.

▶ Yellow Ochre laid over the bodies of the mushrooms and shadow modifies the blue underwash, making it into an interesting warm grey.

you can be braver in your use of colour. All colours mixed together make brown or grey. With watercolour you are effectively 'mixing' by overlaying coloured layers. Therefore, although you may be painting with a bright colour it will be modified by the colour underneath or on top. As a painter you are not obliged to copy the colours of the material world, but can approximate to or even change colours as you wish.

Be brave

Do not be afraid of colour. Timidity never made successful paintings. You can always dull down a painting later on, but if you lose vibrancy at the start it is hard to retrieve it. No colour is wrong in itself; it is only in relation to others that it might not look right. Only when it is down on the paper does instinct tell you it needs perhaps to be more blue, or less bright. The beauty of watercolour is that then you can alter it, overlaying it with a tint of blue or a thin wash of its complementary to dull it down.

Vibrant watercolour paintings are not made up of wishy-washy colours. Think before you paint. Be positive in your choice of colour, definite in your mixes and bold in your application.

◀ **Boats in Burano**
38 x 56 cm (15 x 22 in)
Boats are often brightly painted. They are a great subject for practising brave colour. Here the hulls and reflections merge together wet-in-wet.

Seizing the Moment

By now you will be itching to make some paintings. No doubt you have seen something that sets the visual juices flowing, but you are not feeling brave enough to try a finished picture.

This is where a sketchbook can come to the rescue. It starts off as being a handy way to record things you see and to make instant paintings without regard to composition or finish. It often ends up containing the most vibrant examples of an artist's work, because it is not trying to be anything else. Choose a sketchbook that fits into your life. A size that pops into the pocket, handbag, or briefcase, or that wedges behind your belt, is ideal.

A practical sketchbook

Hardback sketchbooks tend to have a lasting appeal because once filled they can sit happily on a bookshelf for easy retrieval. You can date them on the spine and build up a visual diary of your life. Softback sketchbooks are usually slimmer, with the

▼ Go out with a sketchbook and make quick paintings of scenes and incidents that appeal. Painting is a 'doing' word – you do not improve by just thinking about it!

a gaggle of gulls Aldeburgh.

advantage that you can easily remove leaves of paper, either to frame up your successful sketches, or to give away as gifts.

Whatever you choose, use it. Make some written as well as visual notes while waiting for people, on the bus, in the café. Care not what the finished result looks like. Examine with the eyes, interpret with the brush.

Exercising the eye

Vibrant watercolours come from inside just as much as from outside. How you react to what you see is crucial to the success of your painting. If you cannot see the shadow from a pot, for instance, as integral to that pot you will paint it separately and the painting will look disjointed. Use your sketchbook to stretch your vision. Notice how different units combine together. Look at the shapes of the spaces between objects, rather than the things themselves. All this can be practised in the sketchbook on a small and unembarassing scale.

Collecting reference

Sometimes you will be able to use your sketches to help make larger paintings. In that case you may need to make colour notes on the sketches themselves. There are no rules, everything is permissible.

Using the camera as a sketchbook can also be helpful for freezing quick movements and drawing specific shapes. Painting from photographs is not a very good way to learn, because the camera cannot see in the same way that you do. It treats everything as equally important whereas you home in on something particular. However, once you are confident at painting from life, you will probably find the photograph a useful reference tool.

Above all, using a sketchbook keeps you visually well tuned. If you are not in a position to paint regularly it will at least maintain the momentum.

▶ Cats move quickly, so a size 3 brush loaded with black ink and a small pot of water ready to dilute it are all you need to explore their shapes.

◀ Even a simple sketch of a child's toy in a hotel room carries so much weight in years to come. When I drew this I was just passing time, but now my son is older the sketch actually marks the passing time.

181

The Heart of the Subject

For a painting to be vibrant the subject need not be profound. The most interesting paintings often have very humble subject matter. Think of Van Gogh's chair, Mona Lisa's smile, or Chardin's apples – they are all vibrant paintings of very simple subjects. These paintings catch our imagination because they convey the essence of the subject, even although it may be just a fleeting moment.

Keep it simple

While you are learning to paint keep the subject of your paintings simple and direct. If you are painting a landscape, then place yourself in it. Look around. Ask yourself what interests you? It could be the shape of the tree trunk or the long shadows in stripes on the grass. It may be the bleaching effect of the sun as it strips colour from the edges it strikes. In a still life it might be the tiny gap between the handle of a sugar bowl and a jug, or the light bouncing out of a rim.

The subject in question

Some subjects, such as beautiful scenery or exciting colours, have a more universal appeal than others. Beginners to painting are often drawn towards these subjects as they reap such pleasure from them in 'real life' and long to be able to represent them on

paper. However, these are often quite challenging compositions. So how do you tackle them?

First you need to decide what the actual subject of your painting is. Simply ask yourself, 'What do I like best about this scene?', 'What has attracted me?'. It might be the light, the atmosphere, the small houses against the sky, a particular tree or one colour found among others in a bunch of

▶ **The Breeze**
30 x 20 cm (11 x 8 in)
In the house opposite my studio was a little window with a net curtain. One day the lower sash window was lifted and a gentle breeze caught the net. Suddenly I wanted to paint that window, but the subject was not the window itself; it was the effect of the breeze upon it.

flowers. Once you have chosen your subject the scene becomes the vehicle for drawing attention to this interest. The artist, you, will bring to the viewers' attention something they might not have noticed before, or something you have seen or felt but never crystallized in words.

The main attraction

Whatever the subject is, jot it down beside the painting to remind yourself as you go along. Start your painting or sketch with the main interest, maybe just faintly mapped in, but noted from the outset. As you build up your painting ask yourself continuously is this still the main event, have you focused on it, or have you given equal emphasis to other elements that now distract from it?

It may sound exaggerated to suggest all else surrenders to this subject, but it actually makes it much easier on the artist. If you are painting the light falling on the window beside a vase of flowers, there will come a point when you have painted that light reasonably successfully. Then you will hear a voice inside your head say, 'But more detail is needed in the flowers', or 'The line of the vase is not accurate'. Ask yourself if these things are interfering with the painting of the light. If not, they are best left alone and the painting is finished.

Overworking a painting is a problem that all artists face. Knowing when to stop is much easier if you set yourself a goal and recognize when you have reached it.

▶ **Lazy Morning**
56 x 41 cm (22 x 16 in)
The subject of this painting is not the sofa, the geraniums or the newspaper, but the light streaming through the window – that glorious summer light that steals the colour from the surface on which it falls. The corner of the sunlit room is the vehicle chosen to express that light.

▶ **Sea Horses**
30 x 38 cm (12 x 15 in)
The attraction of this painting was not the horses, or the place, but a wonderful hazy atmosphere felt at dawn by the sea. To keep the sense of mood intact I simplified the background mountains and the waves, and merely suggested details on the riders and their steeds.

◀ **The Shadow**
56 x 76 cm (22 x 30 in)
▼ **The Palm and its Shadow**
76 x 56 cm (30 x 22 in)
The dramatic shadow of the palm tree was my subject in these two pictures. In the painting on the left I emphasized just that. However, I became fascinated with the fronds of the palm tree itself, and as I could not fit them into my composition I started again with the paper turned vertically. Changing one's mind is the artist's prerogative!

Changing your mind

A painting takes place over time, however short, and sometimes as you look and paint the main interest changes. You may start off excited by one particular element, but as you explore the subject visually something else takes on a greater interest. That is fine. You are in charge of the painting, and you can change your mind, but you must follow your thoughts through. A painting about everything is confusing. The viewer looks and thinks, 'Yes, attractive scene, but what is the painting about?' Unless the viewer can sense that you have an interest beyond the obvious physical subject of the painting they will probably be unmoved. Though they may be impressed by your talent or effort they will probably feel uninspired.

Your painting must stand alone from the subject when it is finished. You are free to emphasize or neglect whatever you think works best for the painting's success.

184

Subtlety and ambiguity

Sometimes your interest will be obvious; at other times less so. Subtlety and ambiguity are two of watercolour's most engaging assets. To suggest rather than state allows the viewer to participate. Watercolour's wet-on-dry veils and wet-in-wet blends encourage mystery. Loose brush marks can say so much. Use these attributes to encourage the viewer to become involved.

Integrity

The beauty of painting is that to different people one painting may mean different things. Here is the wonderful paradox of painting: if you are true to your own integrity, painting what you want the way you want, your painting will probably have more appeal than if you try to please other people instead of yourself.

▲ Sometimes you might try to tackle subjects that are less physical. This was the sketch for some canvas paintings about the intimacy between a mother and a child. I feel that this Sepia wash caught that tenderness with a few strokes of the brush.

◄ Red Splash
20 x 28 cm (8 x 11 in)
A simple subject is brought alive by the merging colours, brisk brush strokes and lack of definition. No item is painted precisely but we know exactly what is represented.

Creative Composition

Paintings can be vibrant and lively simply because the composition is successful. Composition is the design of the painting upon the paper. A little forethought and planning can make a painting much more effective, so, before you even begin, decide if the actual piece of paper you are going to use is the right shape and the right size for the picture you want to make.

Having chosen your surface, next plan the layout of the image on the paper.

Viewfinder

Using a viewfinder really helps in planning a painting. Two L-shaped pieces of card placed together to make a variable rectangle are ideal. Hold these out in front of you to form a rectangular window and view your chosen subject through this. Remind yourself of the real subject, the reason for your interest in this particular scene or group of objects. Move the viewfinder around, and back and forth, until you feel a satisfactory balance in the arrangement bounded by the edges of the card. If the view does not readily make a satisfactory composition be prepared to move objects in your actual painting. Do not become such a slave to the view that your painting suffers. The painting comes first.

Three into two does go

A representational painting is a two-dimensional image of a three-dimensional subject. In planning your composition,

◀ To experiment with composition I rearranged this group of objects several times. One advantage of painting the same subject in different arrangements is that it prevents you overworking any one painting, but gives you a chance to enjoy the subject over a longer period of time.

▶ San Giorgio from Schiavoni

41 x 56 cm (16 x 22 in) The focal point of this painting is the church in the distance. The lines of the gondolas lead the eye towards this, but not so blatantly that the composition becomes too obvious.

therefore, you need only look at the two-dimensional arrangement of the shapes, colours, lines and spaces of the view in front of you. The very fact that you desire to paint means you are probably already visually aware of naturally good compositions as they occur around you. Trust your own judgement as to when you think the image looks interesting or balanced.

Focal point

Most paintings benefit from a main focal point of interest in order to draw the viewer's attention. It could be a specific item or a general incident, and is usually the subject of the painting. As you look through the viewfinder move the main interest of your painting to either side of the centre line and up and down. In general a feature of interest looks more dynamic away from the centre. Likewise in a landscape the horizon is better placed either above or below the horizontal centre-line of the painting. If it helps, look at some paintings you admire and then transfer their compositions to your own subject matter.

Sketching your composition

Remember you are only concerned at this stage with a two-dimensional surface. Imagine your viewfinder has a glass pane. If you could trace the view beyond it on to the glass that would be a similar design to the drawing you want on the paper.

Point your finger into the viewfinder at the focal point. Find the equivalent position on your paper and make a dot. Start your drawing from there.

You do not need a highly detailed drawing for most watercolour painting. The sketch should be a guide for the brush simply to tell it where it can and cannot go. Sketch loosely so that you can change your mind with little or no erasure. View your sketch at a short distance to make sure you are happy with the design before you go any further.

▶ Conservatory

76 x 56 cm (30 x 22 in) The subject of this painting is the diffuse light in a glass room rather than any particular items in the conservatory. If your subject is general rather than specific you can still use the composition to lead the eye into the painting.

▶ It can be hard for beginners to accept how small a figure in the distance will be beside a figure in the foreground.

▶ **In the Shadow of Nelson's Column**
28 x 20 cm (11 x 8 in)
By holding a pencil to measure the size of the foreground pigeons and then comparing it with the size of the pigeons in the background the relative proportions are easily found.

Relative scale

Once you have arranged your composition loosely on the paper you can be more specific with the shapes and sizes of the items you portray. Keep in mind the chief inspiration for your painting and still use this as your starting point as you add detail and correct or enhance the drawing. By cross-referring with imaginary horizontal and vertical lines from one object to another you can find and plot the position of everything in relation to the main feature.

Hold your pencil out in front of you and measure the close and distant items in relation to the length of the pencil. By comparing their sizes you will see the difference in scale clearly. The age-old joke of the artist squinting with one eye at his outstretched thumb is none other than this method of measuring!

By cross-reference you will automatically achieve the right scale for various items.

The shapes in between

The shapes between items are as vital to the flat two-dimensional world of the paper as the size and shape of objects themselves. Some artists term these 'negative' shapes, but

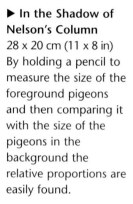

▲ Find the correct curve of the handles on a cup and jug by drawing the shape of the gaps between the body and the handle of each item.

▶ It is much easier to draw the limbs of a figure if you first assess the angles and shape between those limbs. The pose will then quickly fall into place.

▲ Try to see in shape rather than line. This unfinished sketch defines the shapes of the girls on the bench by painting the spaces between and around them.

they are just as important as the shapes inside objects and seeing them clearly will make drawing much easier. When someone stands with their elbow bent and their hand on their waist, look at the shape of the space made between the arm and the body. In the landscape look for the shapes between buildings and under trees.

To practise this, set yourself the task of defining a whole composition by drawing only the shapes in between items and not the actual items themselves.

Check the overall shapes of objects, figures, fields etc. by using the outstretched pencil method to compare the height of an object with its width. Adjust your drawing to compensate for errors of judgement.

Linking shapes

Grouped subjects look more coherent if they are bound together by invisible lines. We do not see things separately, but as parts of a whole. Use the same vision in your painting.

Viewing your painting in a mirror enables you to see errors of drawing more easily.

▲ **Rush Hour**
13 x 18 cm (5 x 7 in)
Instead of seeing objects as separate entities attach them together by merging colours, either by working wet-in-wet or overlaying linking washes. Subjects and their shadows often dissolve one into another. Highlights, too, will blur the lines of separation.

189

Suggesting Form and Space

Creating the illusion of the third dimension on a two-dimensional plane is one of the most exciting aspects of painting. Even after years of painting, I still find it utterly magical that I can start with a blank sheet of paper and end up with something that has its own life.

Making objects look three-dimensional is easier than you think. As we are used to seeing things in the round in our physical world, it takes very little to suggest that something in your painting has three-dimensional form. From experience the viewer already presumes it has.

There are two main ways of creating form. One is by outline and shape, whereas the other is through the use of tone.

The outline

How do you draw a round object on a flat piece of paper? Look again through your viewfinder, and imagine it as a pane of glass. Trace the lines describing the surfaces of objects turning away from you and see how they tilt up or down on the flat picture plane. Use your pencil to find their angles, holding it parallel to the viewfinder. These angles are governed by the laws of perspective, but you need not study perspective to be able to assess the angle of tilt correctly. The information is all in front of you; you only have to copy exactly what you see.

You will notice that at your eye-level the lines are all straight, but as they fall below your eye-level they tilt up towards it, and as they rise above your eye-level they tilt down towards it. By accurate observation and cross-referencing to other items you can find how steeply or gently the lines tilt. Copy these angles as closely as possible on to the

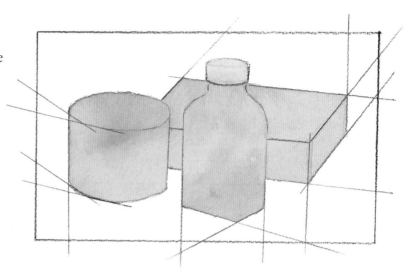

flat paper and you will see the forms taking shape in perspective and looking three-dimensional. The more you observe and practise the easier this becomes.

Variation of tone

With your drawing you may have suggested roundness or bulk with the curve or angle of the line, but you have at your disposal an even more persuasive tool – tone. Tone is the lightness or darkness of an object.

Tone is described by a scale ranging from white through greys to black. Thus a dark tone would be a dark grey, and a light tone a pale grey. When colour is added to tone the

▲ Outline: By copying the tilt of the lines on the flat picture plane, outlines can be built up and three-dimensional form is suggested.

▼ Tone: The outline drawing of these items gives no clue that they are solid forms, but the variation of tone across the surfaces persuades us that the objects are not flat.

▲ Outline and Tone: If we put together a drawing outline that suggests form and paint a variation of tone that suggests form we are convinced that these forms are three-dimensional.

same scale of lightness and darkness occurs within the range of the colour. Even though a ball might be the colour red, around its circumference several different tones of red will be at play. Using this differentiation of tone from the local colour (the perceived colour of the object) enables the artist to suggest its form.

Light source

When an object is lit from one source, such as the sun or a lamp, light falls directly on one surface, but leaves the others in varying degrees of shadow. The side upon which no light falls may be very dark. If there is a lot of ambient light around then these unlit sides will receive a measure of reflected light from all around, but will still be darker than the side facing the light.

When you are planning your composition, bear in mind the source of light. A view with the light source directly in front will not have such an interesting variation of tone as if the light source comes from the side, or slightly behind. Morning and evening will also give you more interesting lights and shadows than a subject that is painted under a noonday sun.

▼ Rock Painting
53 x 74 cm (21 x 29 in)
The strong light source from above lights the top of the rocks, while the sides are given a colourful mid tone. The darkest tones are used in the crevices under the rocks. Just three tones convince us easily of the solidity of these rocks while the colours create the soft ethereal nature of the place.

▶ Imagine three similar-sized trees, each further away, on a road leading to the horizon. If you draw a line across the top and bottom those lines will meet at the horizon. The diminishing size tells us that the trees are receding in space.

Space and distance

Creating the illusion of space in a painting is also about perspective. The horizon is always at eye-level, and all lines leading away from the eye eventually meet at the horizon. Similar-sized objects as they recede look smaller in relation to each other (see the section on 'Relative scale' on page 188). Thus objects and figures in the foreground will appear larger than their equivalents in the background. The viewer has no trouble believing this because they have seen it in real life. You need, therefore, only put the suggestion into their mind and use this fact to enhance the perception of space in your paintings. The greater the difference in size, the more distance suggested.

▼ Fields at Harvest
20 x 28 cm (8 x 11 in)
The relative size of the foreground trees to the ones in the middle distance and those at the horizon convinces the viewer that this is a large open space.

◀ The three trees are all the same size and on the same picture plane, but by lightening the tone from left to right we suggest that the two lighter ones are receding. Likewise, the hills appear to recede into the distance as the tones become paler. Overlapping objects enhances this illusion.

Using tone and colour

We have already seen how powerfully tone describes form, but you can also use tone to suggest distance. Strong dark colours seem to jump forward, while pale colours recede. Therefore, if you paint the far distance lighter than the foreground you will persuade the viewer that space exists within your painting, creating the illusion of depth on the flat paper. Practise comparing the colour of distant hills, mountains or buildings when out in the landscape. They may seem dark in relation to the sky, but if you half close your eyes and match them against something dark in the foreground, you will see how much darker that nearer item will be.

Colour can also help you create space. Reds assert themselves, whereas blues recede. However, since no colour exists without tone (its lightness or darkness) ultimately tone is the more powerful painting tool.

Carry a piece of black card in your pocket and use it to compare the darks and mid tones of the subject you are painting.

◀ **The Long White Beach**
28 x 36 cm (11 x 14 in)
All the artist's tools of illusion are brought into play to suggest the length of this very long beach on the flat surface of paper that is no larger than a window pane. The dramatically diminishing size of the rocks suggests great distance, the paler background tones of the hills recede and the warm foreground colours of the rocks jump forward. Perspective, tone and colour – what a trio!

193

The Power of Contrast

Now that you have used tone to suggest three-dimensional form and the illusion of depth, you will realize how important it is in the structure of a painting. The greater the contrast of tone within an image, the more vibrant and dramatic the final visual effect.

A strong directional light source causes strong tonal contrasts. Bright light through a door throws the rest of the room into shadow. A form lit from behind becomes a silhouetted shape of light against dark. This strong contrast of light and dark transferred to your watercolour makes an arresting painting. A sense of drama is intrinsic in the dark and lightness portrayed.

▲ **Chelsea Arts Club**
18 x 13 cm (7 x 5 in)
An ordinary subject of a jacket draped over the back of a chair is transformed into a vibrant little painting by the dramatic shaft of light cast across the restaurant floor.

Mixing dark colours

To create lively dark areas in your painting, forget ready-made colours such as Black or Payne's Grey. Instead make those dark tones out of two opposite colours, such as blues and browns, or reds and greens. The effects will be rich, dark, slightly variable washes that are full of mystery.

The combinations are endless, and the colours delicious. Mix lots of pigment with enough water to make a creamy mixture. But take care that it is not too thick or you may find that an unwanted sheen appears on the dried surface of the wash.

Remember that very wet watercolour dries lighter than it appears when wet. So, if you think your wash is going to dry too light and it is still wet, plunge more pigment into the wash wet-in-wet.

These darks can be built up in layers, but too many layers will deaden the colour, so try to reach the colour you desire with your first or second wash.

◄ Here are some suggested combinations to make vibrant darks.
Top row: French Ultramarine and Burnt Sienna, French Ultramarine and Burnt Umber, French Ultramarine and Sepia, French Ultramarine and Raw Umber.
Middle row: Prussian Blue and Burnt Sienna, Prussian Blue and Burnt Umber, Prussian Blue and Sepia, Prussian Blue and Raw Umber.
Bottom row: Indigo and Sepia, Crimson Alizarin and Indigo, Crimson Alizarin and Viridian.

The highlights

It is the difference between the light and dark that counts in a painting using tonal contrast, so pay close attention to the lightest areas. The white paper will always represent your lightest highlights. Demarcate those areas you want to remain white in your preliminary sketch and be careful not to paint over them by mistake.

To make the brightest highlights stand out in your paintings, other light areas can be tinted with thin transparent washes to help lessen their brightness.

Shadows

Shadows, like the dark areas in a painting, also benefit from being coloured rather than grey. At sunset the blue or mauve cast to a shadow is very obvious, but even during the day shadows are tinted with colour. It behoves the artist to seek out and emphasize these colours, even if at first you do not believe you see them. Watercolour has the advantage of being transparent, enabling you to lay tints of colour over other colours and thus create coloured shadows that can, if necessary, be modified by other colours on top or that shine through from underneath. Remember that overlaying three primary colours will turn them to greys and browns.

▲ Beachcombing
23 x 15 cm (9 x 6 in)
I love to paint silhouettes against the setting sun. I used masking fluid to hold back the highlights of the sparkles on the water from the all-over Yellow Ochre and Indigo wash.

◄ Singing the Blues
76 x 56 cm (30 x 22 in)
The warmth of French Ultramarine is used to paint the shadows of the flowers and pillow. Contrasted with the stronger French Ultramarine of the cornflowers and the bright yellow chrysanthemums there is no need to modify the blue towards a grey; it already settles back to become a believable shadow.

195

Colour contrast

Contrast is not just about tone. By contrasting opposite or complementary colours you can also achieve dynamic effects. For a vibrant, colourful watercolour, try contrasting red with green, purple with yellow or orange with blue.

These contrasts need not be blatant; remember that subtlety and suggestion are very persuasive. An orange flower set in green foliage that veers to blue will be more striking, and look more orange, than if the foliage green veers to yellow. Use the temperature of colours to create contrast

too. Warm reds placed against cool blues will look hotter than cool reds against warm blues. A painting of a blue sky against a warm Yellow Ochre beach will look brighter than if you paint the beach with a cold Lemon Yellow.

Vibrant greys

For mid greys, try mixing the two-colour combinations suggested on page 194, and dilute with more water. Sometimes you will obtain a wonderful granulating effect as the two colours separate grain from grain on the surface of the paper. This adds texture to the

▼ **Paradise Found**
56 x 76 cm (22 x 30 in)
Africa is hot – the hippos are returning to water. I have used the dramatic contrast of yellow and purple to evoke the excitement I felt at this scene.

▲ Danube Delta
20 x 25 cm (8 x 10 in)
This vast expanse of water and marsh fascinated me. By lowering my eyeline I could break up the soft wet-in-wet wash with angular grasses to bring the sketch to life.

shadow. French Ultramarine and Burnt Sienna will often do this, as will Coeruleum or Manganese Blue and Yellow Ochre, but it does not always happen!

Greys made from two colours will have more character than ready-made greys. You can easily veer them towards the colour you perceive the grey to be – for example, a blue-grey or a green-grey – by adding more of that particular colour in the mix.

Contrast of shape and line

Within a painting contrasts of every kind serve to enhance their opposite number. We have looked at contrast of tone and colour. What about contrast of shape and line?

A painting of soft undefined areas can lack interest, but if you introduce a contrasting angular shape the soft forms

come alive. A landscape view of horizontal fields may well be attractive enough, but the vertical addition of a tree makes the composition sing.

These points may seem obvious when you see a naturally interesting view, but there will be times when you need to bring them to mind deliberately to make the composition lively. You may wish to paint a particular scene and you want it to be authentic to the physical nature of the place but the composition is boring. Try lowering your eyeline by sitting on the ground, so that foreground features rise up to cross the horizon and create a greater contrast of shape or line against the landscape. Look for ways that could make the painting more interesting. Trust your own judgement. If the composition interests you it will almost certainly interest someone else too.

Evoking Atmosphere and Mood

Vibrant watercolours can be strong and vital, exuding excitement, or they can be full of presence, atmosphere and calm. They can even reflect anxiety or foreboding.

How do we create a particular mood or atmosphere in the two-dimensional realm of the painting? It is possible to create atmosphere by using colours and techniques that affect the viewer's emotional response to the image. Not everyone reacts in the same way to the same stimuli, but there are colours that cheer and colours that quiet,

effects that are gentle on the eye and effects that excite or jar. These qualities alone will not make the painting work, however. They need to be supplemented by the artist's own emotional or spiritual input to truly inspire.

The effect of colour

In 'Confident Colour' we discovered that reds are generally active and blues more passive. Strong colours advance, while pale colours recede. These properties can be used

▼ **The Blue Lagoon**
30 x 38 cm (12 x 15 in)
The calmness pervading this painting is encouraged by the use of blue and the soft wet-in-wet blending of colours. I was in a peaceful mood when I painted it and felt a certain clarity in what I was doing. My mood has entered the painting.

by the artist to enhance the mood in the painting. If you want to create a cool, gentle atmosphere veer your overall colour scheme towards a harmony of greens and blues. Avoid too much strong tonal contrast without making your painting insipid. If you want drama and vitality use strong colours and contrast light and dark tones.

This is where you can employ the temperatures of colours to best effect. Keep asking yourself questions such as, 'Does this colour lean towards red or blue?', or 'Is it warm or cool?'. Just by varying the blue from a cool blue, such as Prussian Blue, to a warm blue, such as French Ultramarine, can change the whole mood of the painting.

Limit your palette

One of the problems for beginners is that they often use too many different colours within one painting and so dilute the properties of individual colours. Just because they are there in your palette does not mean that all the colours need to be used for each painting. Start by minimizing the colours used in any one painting. In a sky, for example, decide if you want to create a warm atmosphere or a cooler mood. If the former, choose a warm blue such as Cobalt or French Ultramarine; if cooler, use Prussian and continue the use of that blue throughout the painting.

▲ St Tropez
20 x 28 cm (8 x 11 in)
I wanted to create the 'tired' heat at the end of a hot Mediterranean day. To suggest warmth with a touch of the coming coolness of evening I chose Crimson Alizarin, a cool red. The only other colours I used were Yellow Ochre (warm) and French Ultramarine (warm). Using few colours guarantees the unity of the painting.

199

◄ **Heartbeat of Africa**
56 x 76 cm (22 x 30 in)
Light has temperature.
A warm light needs a
warm colour, so you
could use Yellow
Ochre, as in this
painting, for an
underwash. While it
was still wet I blended
the mauves of the
distant trees into the
ochre wash. The effect
not only suggests heat
but also rising dust.

Coloured light

White paper is perfect for portraying the
light of broad daylight, but a painting made
at dawn or sunset, or in a firelit interior,
needs an overall cast of colour to convince
the viewer it is painted under a coloured
light. To create this effect you can tint the
whole paper at the outset with an overall
pale wash of the colour you perceive the
light to be, and then, when thoroughly dry,
paint on top, leaving the lightest highlights
as the tinted paper. This underwash of
colour helps create the ambient light or
atmosphere, and can be used to suggest a
general warmth or coolness in a painting
right from the start. You could also work
on coloured watercolour paper.

Mix plenty of colour to a dilute wet
consistency. Wet the paper first for a more
even flow, then lay the colour with broad
strokes so that each stroke merges wet-in-
wet with the one before. Use spotlessly clean
water to mix these transparent tints. Do not
fiddle with the wash as it dries; any irritating

imperfections will later disappear under the
layers of painting on top.

Understatement and suggestion

One of the most intriguing qualities of
watercolour is that more can often be said
by suggestion than by detailed description.

▼ A cool light needs
a cool colour. Here I
have laid an overall
wash of pale Prussian
Blue and Coeruleum to
create the atmosphere
of wintry sunshine.

200

A few loose brush strokes at the horizon can make someone believe a whole mountain range exists. The more the viewer puts their own interpretation and imagination into your painting, the more involved and interested they will become.

To create mystery in a painting, use the wet-in-wet technique. Let the colours dissolve together, so that shadows and the objects that cast them dissolve together with indefinable edges. Allow the features in the distance to merge and let the clothes on a figure blend into the flesh. Do not try to exert too much control over all your washes. By limiting the flow of the watercolour, you may be denying your painting the very life it craves. If a little paint runs into some unintended area, do not automatically assume that it will ruin your painting; on the contrary, it may well enhance it.

▼ A wash of Burnt Sienna, a few darker blobs across the middle and some upward streaks in the foreground: how little we need do with watercolour to suggest a landscape.

▼ **A Breath of Colour** 38 x 56 cm (15 x 22 in) Look closely at this painting of anemones and see how little actual detail has been painted. The edges of the flowers are often blurred with wet-in-wet washes and thin wet-on-dry veils of colour suggest overlapping petals. Everything is understated, yet perfectly understood, and a gentle atmosphere prevails.

Brush stroke and gesture

Using different papers and different brushes will help to create atmosphere and exciting effects, but more often than not it is the actual gesture of the brush stroke that contributes to the energy of the painting.

Paint, loosely applied, will create a livelier atmosphere than a painting made with stiff, nervous brush strokes. The life and character of brushwork is largely due to confidence.

The more you paint, the fewer brush strokes you will lay, and the more meaningful each brush stroke will become.

Sometimes what appears as abandon on the part of the artist is, in fact, quite carefully thought out. These brush strokes have only been laid when the right colour was mixed to the right consistency and aimed at the right place. The gesture may appear spontaneous, but it is actually loaded with thought and preparation.

▶ **Juarati**
56 x 43 cm (22 x 17 in)
In this painting the washes are allowed a measure of freedom. I worked with a large sable brush with a good point, sweeping the paint on in meaningful brush strokes. The rough paper adds the thrilling element of texture.

◄ **Evening Stroll**
18 x 25 cm (7 x 10 in)
There is an air of mystery to this evening stroll along the beach. The confidence of the dry-brush strokes contrasts well with the loose wet-in-wet washes and the figures and their reflections are put in boldly with a quick flick of the tip of the brush.

▼ If you choose subjects that you love you will see that genuine affection come out in the painting. Try making sketches of your family and friends doing things they enjoy.

Character

The spirit with which you paint will imbue the painting. If you are happy and relaxed the painting will have that joy and lightness of spirit. If you are frustrated and dissatisfied, the painting will be lacklustre too. You do not need to be 'in the mood' to paint, however. You can start a painting feeling wholly separate from it and yet as you progress you will become completely involved. It is your commitment to the painting that counts. The more you put into a painting, not in terms of detail, but in observation, concentration, decision, animation and love, the more integrity your painting will have.

If you are painting indoors, listening to music while you paint can also affect and enhance the mood of your painting.

Freedom of Movement

The portrayal of movement within a painting can liven up any composition. Swift brush strokes and blurred edges suggest activity. If you are including people in a scene, painting their shapes as if they are in the process of moving looks far more interesting than static figures. Even if their shapes seem inaccurate you will be surprised at how much you can get away with just by suggesting movement. The eye will complete the action.

Sketching moving subjects

Practise sketching and painting moving figures in a sketchbook. Then, when you need them for a finished painting, you can copy them on to the watercolour with more confidence. As you sketch with a brush or a pencil keep your eye on the subject rather than constantly looking down at your paper.

It is undoubtedly harder to draw a subject when it is moving than when it is still. When I am painting wild animals in Africa, instead

◄ In these figures, sketched while out shopping, movement is suggested by painting one foot shorter than the other, by joining the legs together in a 'V', or inverting the 'V' to imply walking.

▼ **On the Move**
20 x 56 cm (8 x 22 in)
Wet-in-wet is perfect for the backgrounds of moving subjects. It gives the impression of blur, and therefore suggests that the objects in front are moving. Note how the limbs of the animals fade out towards their extremities.

of following the changing movements of one animal I look for another that has taken up a similar position. Herd animals and people in groups repeatedly echo the positions of their peers.

Look for the pattern of the legs, and rather than finish the leg off with the finality of a foot, leave the end of the leg indistinct.

Photographs to the rescue

Since the famous photographs of equine motion taken by Eadweard Muybridge at the end of the nineteenth century the camera has proved to be an invaluable tool when painting movement. With it you can catch the immediacy of moving shapes and transfer them to your paintings. Some actions happen too fast even to sketch; here the camera is invaluable. If you are working from photographs, however, beware making your figures look static within their movement. Still remember to blur a little or leave something slightly unfinished or indistinct. Try to imagine you are actually painting from life and the figure is about to change position. Put pressure on yourself to

work fast so that the brush stroke will retain its original energy and spontaneity.

Suggestion of activity

Even still life and flower paintings can benefit from a hint of movement. Shadows move and light dances, petals lift and fall. Letting colours spread wet-in-wet into the background gives the appearance of momentary movement. Thin washes that extend beyond the edges of the objects suggest an adjustment in the parallax of the eye and indicate time passing. If your painting looks too static wet the areas beside hard edges and encourage or drag the colour into the surrounding area to blur the edge.

◀ To paint the swiftly moving horses I loaded the brush with Sepia ink and laid a quick brush stroke for the leading horse. I then added water to my brush and painted the second horse so that the washes blurred slightly together, wet-in-wet. The drawing does not need to be accurate to suggest movement.

Puddle in the Kings Road.

◀ **A Bigger Splash**
46 x 66 cm (18 x 26 in)
To create the splash from the puddle I painted masking fluid in energetic brush strokes, following the movement of the water as it careered up from either side and in front of the taxi. This was rubbed off when the painting was dry and touched in with directional brush strokes in places.

205

Textures and Surfaces

Surface textures are not only great fun to paint but they also look wonderful in watercolour. To paint every last detail of an intricate texture is extremely absorbing, but it is time consuming, so I am going to suggest a few textural techniques that are quick and easy to do and look very effective.

Sponging

The irregular surface of a natural sea sponge is marvellous for painting speckled textures such as light foliage, granite, gravel, flower centres or sprays of tiny flowers. Mix up plenty of paint to a creamy solution and dab the sponge into the mix. Press the loaded sponge on to the area to be painted to make speckles in a lovely random pattern. Build up the patina with different colours, letting each layer dry before patting on the next.

Salt crystals

An exciting, but slightly unpredictable, texture can be created by sprinkling ground salt crystals into a rich wet wash. The salt

◀ When the background wash is dry green paint is dabbed and patted on to the foliage areas with a sponge. A darker layer is added to create the shadows of the foliage masses. The branches are touched in with a fine brush while the paint is still damp.

◀ The rock forms are loosely differentiated with a shadow blue wash. The granite texture can then be built up with successive layers of sponged colours, keeping the overall tone of the boulders in mind.

◀ **Guardians**
28 x 36 cm (11 x 14 in)
Salt crystals were sprinkled at random into strong wet washes of French Ultramarine, Prussian Blue and Burnt Sienna. When the paint was dry the salt was brushed off the paper with the hand, leaving these lovely patterns in its wake.

absorbs the pigment from the wash and leaves an attractive variety of lichen-like patterns on the paper. Only brush the salt crystals off when completely dry.

Dry-brush

Painting with dry paint or splayed brush hairs is ideal for quickly creating a broken, uneven texture. The end of a brush stroke after it has shed almost all its load will create a dry-brush mark, so exploit this property to create texture in your paintings.

Waxing

The fact that water and oil do not mix provides opportunities for textural effects that the watercolourist can exploit. One of my favourite techniques is to use an ordinary white wax candle. This is perfect both for suggesting a rough texture and for reserving highlights on textured surfaces.

For details, sharpen the end of the candle with a scalpel blade and draw or rub the candle over the highlit area. When you apply paint the waxed area resists the watercolour and a lovely broken edge results, with scattered blobs of colour settling in the tooth of the paper where the wax does not catch. You cannot remove the wax once it is laid, so be certain that you want the waxed area to remain unpainted. I use waxing for texture on rocks, walls, people and foliage.

◀ Wax rubbed over dried paint will reserve areas from the next laid wash. In this sketch wax is rubbed on in several stages beneath successive washes to create an interesting texture and highlights on the surfaces.

▼ **Pebbles on the Beach**
20 x 28 cm (8 x 11 in) Every technique under the sun was applied to this pebble painting. Salt crystals were tossed into a wet-in-wet variegated wash, the stones picked out wet-on-dry and their textures created with dry-brush, sponging, wax and white gouache.

DEMONSTRATION ELEVEN

Al Fresco

Everyday objects are always rewarding to paint and food is no exception. The subject matter comes to life on the paper as the three-dimensional forms become convincing. I arranged the vegetables on the chequered cloth, placing the cauliflower as a backdrop to the smaller forms. To enhance the roundness of the shapes I lit the still-life group from the right.

▶ First stage

Colours

French Ultramarine

Cadmium Red

Indian Yellow

Prussian Blue

Sepia

Yellow Ochre

Crimson Alizarin

First Stage

Having sketched the shapes of the vegetables with an 8B pencil, I half-closed my eyes to ascertain the main lights and darks. I then washed in the areas of shadow with dilute French Ultramarine, using a size 12 sable brush. With this simple tonal wash the forms were already taking shape. I painted masking fluid over the fine trailing roots of the spring onions, so that I could paint freely over them without having to worry about painting round the individual threads.

Second Stage

Next I began to describe the forms with their local colours. I started with a wet wash of Cadmium Red on the tomatoes. Into this I plunged darker colour round the shaded side to enhance the three-dimensional look. I also carried the red into the cloth below, where the redness reflected on the fabric.

While the small orange capsicum was wet I dabbed a touch of red into the Indian Yellow wash, again carrying the colour on to the cloth to show the reflected light. The

◀ Second stage

greens of the pepper, spring onions and cauliflower leaves were made with Prussian Blue and Indian Yellow. For the deliciously dark insides of the mushrooms I used a varying mixture of Sepia, Indian Yellow and Cadmium Red, leaving out thin lines to suggest the gills fanning from the stalk.

Third Stage

Now I could see that the composition and colours were working as a whole I felt confident to work on the three-dimensional form of the individual items. I began by rewetting the centres of the mushrooms with clear water and plunged almost neat Sepia under their rims. A wash of pale Yellow Ochre over the blue on the underside of the back mushroom gave me a suitable warm grey for the slightly dirty-looking white sides.

Then I continued with the tomatoes. I rewetted them from the base, adding Indian Yellow to the top of each tomato and Crimson Alizarin at the bottom.

I now picked a smaller brush, a size 5 sable, for painting around the highlights on the green pepper.

As I worked round the whole cauliflower I suggested veins in the leaves by leaving linear gaps between washes. Indian Yellow mixed with Prussian Blue made marvellous non-garish greens.

◀ Third stage

Finished Stage

The chequered lines of the cloth were painted in stripes of French Ultramarine, first in one direction and then, when those were dry, in the other direction. Painting the checks helped to bring out the bulbs of the spring onions.

I stood back from the painting to see how well the vegetables stood out from the paper. I decided the blues of the cloth needed darkening with a little Crimson Alizarin and a dash of Sepia. Then I emphasized the shadows under all the vegetables until they looked good enough to eat!

◄ **Al Fresco**
28 x 38 cm (11 x 15 in)

Making Hay

The shadows were lengthening on a warm summer's day. I wanted to convey the atmosphere of warmth and the golden light. To create distance and a sense of space in the painting I would make the tones of the hills and the back haystacks lighter than the foreground and use the diminishing size of the haystacks to create perspective.

Colours

Yellow Ochre

Prussian Blue

Crimson Alizarin

Burnt Sienna

◀ First stage

First Stage

To give the picture a pervading atmosphere of warmth I decided to underwash the painting with a warm transparent colour that would shine through, and embrace, all the subsequent washes on top. Over a loose pencil sketch I laid an initial wash of Yellow Ochre using a 16 mm (⅝ in) flat sable brush, blending it wet-in-wet at sky level with pale Prussian Blue. I avoided any temptation to 'fill in' any unpainted areas.

Second Stage

The first wash I laid was a pale mauve-grey made from Yellow Ochre, Crimson Alizarin and Prussian Blue. This created the furthermost hill. When this had dried I painted the next hill with wet-in-wet blends in a variegated wash of the same three colours, but slightly darker and much greener. This suggested woodland and fields. The nearest hill was painted in the same way, leaving the fields to dry before painting

212

◀ Second stage

in the trees with the same mixture but redder and darker to bring the hill closer.

The standing trees at the edge of the field were painted in a mixture of Crimson Alizarin, Yellow Ochre and Burnt Sienna as the hill wash around them was drying. Some of the wash blended wet-in-wet and some overlapped, giving a combination of hard and soft edges. The trunk of the tree was reserved as tinted paper within the wash.

Third Stage

I painted another underwash over the shapes of the haystacks to enrich and unite them in colour before shaping them with tone. I separated the trees and bushes at the edge of the field by touching darker colour into rewetted corners. Over the foreground of the field I washed Burnt Sienna with a 16 mm (⅝ in) flat brush, leaving the initial ochre wash as the areas of sunshine.

▶ Third stage